THE CANCER PREVENTION COOKBOOK

THE CANCER PREVENTION COOKBOOK

OVER 50 DELICIOUS RECIPES TO REDUCE THE RISK OF CANCER

BEATRICE HEYWOOD TAYLOR

LORENZ BOOKS

For Katherine

This edition published in the UK in 1999 by Lorenz Books

Lorenz Books is an imprint of Anness Publishing Limited
Hermes House, 88–89 Blackfriars Road, London SE1 8HA

This edition distributed in Canada by Raincoast Books
8680 Cambie Street, Vancouver, British Columbia V6P 6M9

A CIP catalogue record is available from the British Library

ISBN 0 7548 0231 0

Publisher: Joanna Lorenz
Executive Editor: Linda Fraser
Editor: Susannah Blake
Designer: Ian Sandom
Photographers: Nicki Dowey, Michelle Garrett, Janine Hosegood,
Dave King, William Lingwood, Tom Odulate and Sam Stowell
(Pictures on p21 were supplied by Tony Stone Images)

Printed and bound in Singapore

1 3 5 7 9 10 8 6 4 2

NOTES
For all recipes, quantities are given in both metric and imperial measures
and, where appropriate, measures are also given in standard cups and
spoons. Follow one set, but not a mixture, because they are not
interchangeable.

Standard spoon and cup measures are level.
1 tsp = 5ml, 1 tbsp = 15ml, 1 cup = 250ml/8fl oz

Australian standard tablespoons are 20ml. Australian readers should
use 3 tsp in place of 1 tbsp for measuring small quantities of gelatine,
cornflour, salt, etc.

Medium eggs are used unless otherwise stated.

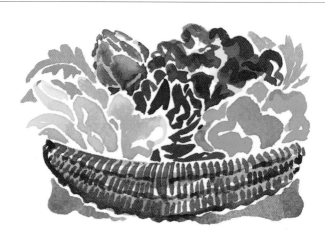

CONTENTS

INTRODUCTION

Historically, conventional medicine has rejected links between cancer and nutrition. However, recent scientific research shows that better nutrition and healthier eating can definitely help both to prevent and treat cancer, which is now the second highest cause of death in the developed world. Cancer is a conquerable disease.

In choosing better foods for healthier living, it is important to select those that not only sustain life but that also renew and regenerate cells and boost the immune system. Eating healthier foods has been shown to reduce the risk of cancer by between 30 and 60 per cent, which are indeed encouraging statistics!

EVOLVING EATING PATTERNS

Before society became industrialized, food came from the land. People ate a balance of meats, dairy produce, cereals and grains, and natural sugar obtained from fruits and vegetables.

In today's busy world, eating patterns have changed dramatically and modern meals are often unbalanced. They tend to be made up largely of dairy produce and animal foods, while valuable plant foods, such as fruits, vegetables, cereals and wholegrains are left out.

Fast food shops are now popular and provide a supply of cooked foods that are too high in fat, sugar and protein. Processed "convenience" foods and ready-made meals, which are full of additives and preservatives, are also common. As a result, people have developed a taste for unhealthy foods.

Cooking with animal fats and some oils is not only unhealthy, but may actually enourage cancer. Eating too much protein makes the body acidic, which may cause free-radical damage to cells.

Over-refined foods, such as white sugar and white flour products, do not replenish or nourish the body. Some nutritionists go even further, believing that sugar is actually a poison, feeding cancer cells and draining the body of important nutrients.

So the messages seems clear, if you want to stay healthy, you need to follow a well-balanced diet of fresh and wholesome foods.

DIETS AROUND THE WORLD

There are groups of people around the world, such as the Hunzas of the Himalayas, the Georgians in Russia, and the Vilcamba of Ecuador, who follow nutritious diets of natural, unrefined foods and often live to be over 100 years of age, and who remain remarkably free of cancer.

The Hunzas' diet, which would appear to lie behind their good health and longevity, consists of rich mineral water; complete proteins of millet, soya beans, barley and buckwheat; natural fibre foods, such as almonds, sesame seeds, leafy green vegetables, berries, peas and freshly sprouted seeds and grains; and enzyme-rich fermented foods, such as yogurt and soured milk.

Similarly, the Seventh Day Adventists in America are vegetarians and have been seen to develop half the number of cases of cancer experienced by the rest of the population.

The Mediterranean diet of tomatoes, olives, onions, garlic, oregano, cold-pressed olive oil and grapes, which is

WHAT CAUSES CANCER?

Cancer develops when abnormal cells divide and multiply, running out of control. These dividing cells form tumours, which can spread relentlessly around the body. Even though thousands of body cells can become malignant every day, a strong immune system can destroy such cells and prevent cancer. Pollution, radiation, smoking and too much sunshine can all cause cancer, but it is believed that many cancers develop as a result of an unhealthy and unbalanced diet.

Soup flavoured with miso, which is derived from the nutrient-rich soya bean.

High-fibre dahl is full of protein and helps speed up the digestive process.

high in natural antioxidants and other nutrients, has also been shown to lower the incidence of cancer.

Asian peoples, who also have low cancer rates, eat many plant foods and plenty of pulses, grains, seeds and nuts. The Indian diet uses very little meat or sugar. Dates, raisins, dried apricots and root vegetables are popular, and dahl, which is made from lentils and is one of the most commonly eaten foods in India, possesses anti-cancer nitrilosides. Green tea, a favourite drink in Asian countries, is becoming popular in the West as a highly antioxidant drink that is believed to help in the fight against cancer. Popular foods consumed in Japan, which are considered to have anti-cancer properties, are soya beans, seaweeds, rice and miso.

It should also be noted that many indigenous peoples, including the Aborigines, Polynesians and North American Indians, did not suffer from cancer until they started to follow the over-refined diet of the West. Copying Western eating habits has proved to be a backward step, underlining the need to use fresh, non-processed foods if we wish to improve our chances of maintaining good health.

THE ANTIOXIDANT THEORY

Research suggests that cancer is caused by an antioxidant deficiency. Foods from plants have been proved to possess cancer-preventing qualities and antioxidant nutrients. These anti-cancer properties may prove to be the best solution to conquering cancer. The key nutrients are: vitamins A, C, D and E, co-enzyme Q_{10}, selenium, manganese, zinc, copper, iron, chromium, lycopene and beta-carotene.

Vitamin A, in its natural form, is found only in animal products, particularly in fish liver and animal liver. It can also be found in lesser amounts in eggs, milk and butter. The beta-carotene in some fruits and vegetables is changed to vitamin A after it has been eaten.

Vitamin E reduces the cells' need for oxygen and is present in dark green vegetables, citrus fruits, seeds, vegetable oils, corn, soya beans, carrots, spinach and apricots. Vitamin E strengthens the immune system. Vitamin C, present in all fresh fruits and vegetables, works with vitamin E to prevent carcinogens forming.

Selenium is a crucial antioxidant nutrient. Although it is present in grains and seeds, depleted soil means that supplementation may be necessary. Other major antioxidant nutrients include iron, manganese, zinc, copper and chromium.

Sulphur-containing compounds, found in cruciferous vegetables like broccoli, are good cancer inhibitors and block the reaction of certain carcinogens with DNA.

Oranges, lemons and kiwi fruit are rich in vitamin C.

Green tea is high in antioxidants and is a powerful anti-cancer drink.

Eggs, milk and butter contain the antioxidant nutrient, vitamin A.

Dark green vegetables, carrots and apricots contain vitamin E.

EATING FOR HEALTH

Being healthy means taking responsibility for your choices about nutrition. Foods can become used as a remedy, alongside conventional and complementary therapies. A positive change to high nutrient foods that truly feed the body can be an exciting challenge. As taste buds adapt, so the body cleanses itself and greater energy and well-being are experienced.

WHAT YOU CAN DO

Begin in a relaxed manner, reducing and cutting out over-refined, processed foods and potentially harmful additives, and opting for fresh, high-antioxidant nutrition. Too many rapid changes may result in the fast elimination of toxins leading to skin reactions and head and body aches, so a measured and informed plan is important.

• Build up a stock of natural and organic wholefoods.
• Develop your own personal anti-cancer nutrition lists.
• Study food labels (take a magnifying glass if necessary!) to avoid processed and additive-ridden foods.
• Eat more raw foods. These contain important enzymes, which help to keep the body healthy, but that are destroyed from the heat of cooking.
• Eat more "live" foods, which contain all the nutrients and enzymes that are essential for health.
• Invest in a powerful juicer and drink fresh vegetable and fruit juices.
• Drink green tea, which is high in anti-cancer nitrilosides.

• Drink eight glasses of low-sodium mineral water each day.
• Learn about growing fresh herbs, sprouting seeds and grains and, the powerful anti-cancer plant, wheatgrass.
• Seek out local farms and outlets for organic foods. Buy fresh from the market, where fruits and vegetables are not wrapped in cellophane.
• Give up white sugar and related foods. After a few weeks, your taste buds will adapt and you won't want sugar any more.
• Cut down on fried foods and avoid hydrogenated products and refined oils and margarines. Processed vegetable fats, including hydrogenated vegetable oils, such as white cooking fats, spreads and margarines, are linked with cancer.
• Use extra virgin olive oil, linseed and sesame oils.
• Eat oily fish, such as sardines, tuna herring, mackerel, salmon and eel, which are rich in omega-3 fatty acids.
• Reduce your consumption of dairy products.
• Boost the good flora in the gut by eating "live" yogurts.

• Cut down on red meats.
• Find an organic meat outlet and favour poultry, which is lower in fat than red meat.
• Focus on complete proteins from plant sources in soya products such as tofu, sprouted seeds, and pulses such as chick-peas and lentils.
• Increase your natural fibre intake, adding cereals, legumes, nuts, fruits and vegetables.
• Avoid white flour products, such as white breads, pies, cakes and biscuits.
• Choose brown rice, buckwheat and millet. Cooked millet contains all the essential vitamins, minerals and amino acids, does not leach the body of vital calcium, and is high in nitrilosides.
• Use garlic and onions regularly.
• Use herbs such as mint, thyme and rosemary, which have a cleansing effect on the body.
• Check the required balance of salt in your diet. The body needs at least half a gram daily, preferably good sea salt.
• Make sure that you eat at least five portions of fresh vegetables and fruits each day.

Fresh vegetable juices and mineral water both hydrate and cleanse your body.

Tofu, lentils and chick-peas are low in fat and a good source of protein.

Onions and garlic contain valuable cancer-fighting phytochemicals.

FOODS TO AVOID

Being aware of all the foods that enter your mouth helps safeguard against eating foods that may be harmful to you.

• Avoid any foods that are burned, charred, rancid or stale.

• Stale foods, such as grains and nuts, can become contaminated with fungi called mycotoxins, thought to cause liver cancer.

• Cut down on fried foods.

• Avoid using hydrogenated and saturated fats and oils found in butters, vegetable fat, margarines and certain oils. Avoid packaged foods that contain these fats.

• Avoid foods that contain artificial colourings, chemicals or additives.

• Cut out white sugar and related products in cereals, sweets, cakes, pies and biscuits. Refined sugars can create mucus that clogs the system and causes constipation.

• If you choose an alcoholic drink, avoid spirits and pick good wines, or organic wines that have not been through a chemical process.

• Try not to eat foods manufactured with added salt.

• Avoid eating refined grains in white bread and white flour. Lack of fibre in these starchy foods can clog the digestive system.

• Cut down on dairy products such as cream, butter, full cream milk, lard and some margarines.

• Check on your protein intake. Too much protein can overload the digestive system.

• Avoid animal protein foods, particularly red meats and cold meats that contain nitrites and other harmful preservatives.

• Check that you have not become a slave to your taste buds and your appetite. Addictions to foods high in sugars and fats, particularly chocolate, sweets and crisps, are common nowadays. Maintaining the correct weight is important – extra fat tissue is believed to make people more vulnerable to cancers.

• Try not to overeat and, instead, end meals still feeling a little hungry.

• Don't rush meals and be sure to chew foods thoroughly.

• However, as well as being aware of what you eat, avoid becoming over-anxious about which foods to choose. Occasional treats can play an important psychological role in maintaining good health.

Above: Foods to avoid include sugary cakes, biscuits and sweets. Top right: Cooking with butter, lard and vegetable fat may encourage cancer. Right: Organic wine, processed without the use of chemicals, makes a healthier choice than spirits.

THE RIGHT FOODS TO EAT

Eating the right foods will provide you with the nutrients required for good health. Aim for balanced meals, using fresh, natural, non-processed foods. Experts favour low-protein, low-calorie, low-fat diets that are high in natural carbohydrates.

Many foods have been highlighted as particularly beneficial in cancer protection. These include fresh fruits and vegetables, oily fish, olive oil, nuts and seeds, soya products, pulses and grains, and drinks that are rich in chlorophyll.

FRUITS AND VEGETABLES

These are seen as the key defence in the fight against cancer. Experts recommend eating between five and seven portions of fruits and vegetables daily. This alone may halve the risk of developing cancer.

Fruits and vegetables are high in fibre and contain many valuable nutrients, including vitamins A, C and E, and folic acid. They also contain powerful phytochemicals, which inhibit the growth of tumours, repair damaged cells and boost the immune system. The most potent anti-cancer fruits and vegetables are watermelon, canteloupe

melon, citrus fruits, berries, tomatoes, broccoli, Brussels sprouts, carrots, garlic, ginger and linseed.

Left: Canteloupe melon, tomatoes, ginger and Brussels sprouts are anti-cancer foods.

FISH AND FISH OILS

Although fish is an important source of protein, the key element in cancer prevention and intervention is the large amount of omega-3 fatty acids that it contains. Oily fish, such as mackerel, herring, sardine, tuna and salmon, are particularly high in these nutrients and some experts recommend eating them two or three times a week.

Fish oils have been shown to stop established cancers spreading and to strengthen the immune system. Fish that are rich in vitamin D are known to slow down cancer: the best source of vitamin D is eel.

Try to obtain fish from clean salt or fresh water sources that are free of pesticides and chemicals. Select smaller fish because they have had less time to absorb toxins. Never eat fish skins because poisonous chemicals may have been deposited there.

BETA-CAROTENE

This powerful antioxidant nutrient is changed to vitamin A in the body. It boosts the immune system and provides oxygen to the body's cells, helping to fight cancer.

Beta-carotene is found in orange, red and yellow vegetables and fruits, such as carrots, apricots, cantaloupe melons and sweet potatoes, and in dark green vegetables such as spinach, broccoli, cabbage and Brussels sprouts. Beta-carotene is especially effective in treating stomach cancer. It has the power to destroy cancer cells and is an important preventative agent. When combined with vitamin E, beta-carotene has an increased anti-cancer effect.

Women who are vulnerable to cervical cancer may be protected by taking a daily supplement of beta-carotene – the suggested intake is between 10,000 and 50,000IU daily – and at least 90mg of vitamin C.

Links have been made between levels of beta-carotene in the diet and the incidence of lung cancer. The carcinogenic dangers of breathing polluted air and tobacco smoke may be reduced by beta-carotene.

Orange-fleshed melons, red and yellow peppers, red sweet potatoes and carrots are rich in beta-carotene.

Oily fish, such as mackerel and herring, are rich in omega-3 fatty acids.

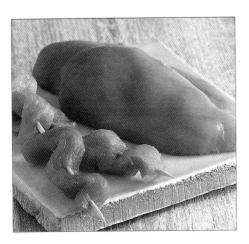

Free-range chicken is a good animal protein choice and has less fat than red meat.

MEAT AND POULTRY

Historically, meat has been linked with strengthening and building the body. But it is high in animal protein and saturated fats, and experts now believe that eating some meats, particularly red ones, can actually increase the chances of developing cancer.

Protein and some of the other vital nutrients provided by meat and poultry can equally well be obtained from complex carbohydrates. It is important to remember that in many societies where there is little or no cancer people eat little or no meat.

Poultry contains less fat than red meat and is easier to digest, but chickens and turkeys that are bred for commercial use are fed with growth hormones and chemicals. Try to buy from farmers who follow free-range and organic processes. Choose lean cuts, or cut off any fat. Avoid prepared cold meats, because these are processed with harmful chemicals.

OILS

A balance of omega-3 and omega-6 essential fatty acids is known to be important for your health. So which oils should you choose?

Restrict omega-6 vegetable oils to sunflower, corn and safflower. Choose cold-pressed olive oil, linseed and rapeseed oils. Linseed and rapeseed oils provide the best balance of essential

fatty acids. Antioxidant olive oils have proven anti-cancer properties. Research has shown that including omega-3 fish oils and olive oil in the diet lowers the rate of breast cancer.

NUTS AND SEEDS

These are a good plant source of protein as well as fibre. They help to provide the body with vital nutrients that can boost the immune system. Sesame seeds also contain generous amounts of calcium.

Nuts have proven anti-cancer properties. Walnuts and almonds, for example, contain the antioxidant oleic acid, while Brazil nuts contain large amounts of selenium, a powerful anti-cancer antioxidant. Walnuts also contain ellagic acid, which is another cancer-fighting antioxidant.

Almost any plant seed can be sprouted. The sprouts, which are loaded with health-giving enzymes and vital nutrients, grow in just a few days.

Above: Choose rapeseed oil, sunflower oil, extra virgin olive oil and linseed oil to obtain essential fatty acids.

Brazil nuts, walnuts and almonds contain powerful antioxidants.

DAIRY PRODUCTS

These foods, which include milk, butter, cream, cheeses, yogurt and ice cream, are sources of protein, vitamin D, sodium and calcium. Anti-cancer diets recommend limiting these foods as they tend to be high in fats, particularly saturated fatty acids, which are thought to increase the risk of many cancers. Cow's milk also contains large amounts of casein, which can clog the digestive system with mucus.

Many of the vital nutrients found in dairy products, such as calcium and protein, can easily be obtained from other sources, such as green vegetables, beans, nuts, sea vegetables, sesame seeds and tahini. Unhydrogenated olive oil margarines are becoming a popular alternative to butter. Goat's milk is a healthy choice for people who have an intolerance to the lactose in cow's milk. Yogurt and fermented milks, such as buttermilk and kefir, are more easily assimilated because fermentation breaks down the lactose. Milk, cheeses and yogurt that come from sheep and goats are available in many shops and are often found to be easier to digest.

SOYA PRODUCTS

Traditional Eastern diets maintain a balance of nutrients through the use of soya beans in conjunction with grains and seaweeds. Soya products are high in protein and low in carbohydrates.

Nutritionists have found that soya products can play an important role in lowering the risk of cancer. Soya beans contain phytochemicals, which help to slow down the rate at which cancer cells divide and allow the body to repair itself.

Many products are produced from soya beans. Tofu and tempeh, which are a mixture of soya beans and rice or barley, are both high in nutrients and low in fat. They are ideal sources of protein and can be eaten instead of meat. Other soya products include soya

Below: Goat's milk, yogurt and cheese are a good choice for people who have an intolerance to lactose.

"milk", "cream" and "yogurt", flour, soy sauce and miso, which is a tasty, fermented paste. Small amounts of miso can be used to flavour soups, sauces and dressings.

Soya flour, tofu, tempeh, and soya "milk" and "yogurt" are rich in protein and can play an important role in lowering the risk of cancer.

PULSES AND CEREALS

In some parts of the world, a mixture of pulses and grains form the basis of the population's diet. These foods provide a rich supply of plant protein, carbohydrates and fibre.

Pulses are high-fibre foods that can speed up the digestive process. There is evidence to suggest that they help to prevent cancer. Popular pulses include soya beans, lentils, chick-peas, black-eyed beans and mung beans.

Cereals, such as wheat bran, have also been shown to reduce levels of cancer by promoting oestrogen in the blood. (However, wheat triggers an allergic reaction in some people.)

Corn and rice are both considered to be anti-cancer grains because they possess protease inhibitors. Rice is thought to be the grain that is the least likely to irritate the immune system. Millet is particularly high in nutrients, and is a key food in populations with a low incidence of cancer.

Above top: A selection of cereals — brown rice, wheat bran and couscous. Above: Peas and beans are high-fibre foods, which speed up the digestive process.

Drinks

Drinking eight glasses of mineral water a day hydrates and cleanses your body.

Green tea and chlorophyll-rich drinks, such as wheatgrass juice, and shakes made with Klamath Lake blue-green algae and Spirulina, are powerful anti-cancer drinks. They cleanse the blood and increase the oxygen supply, preventing free radicals from forming.

Freshly juiced organic vegetable and fruit juices are also recommended as part of a cancer prevention diet. Carrot juice in particular, is believed to have strong anti-cancer properties.

Anti-cancer healing teas are also popular and include horsetail, cat's claw, Pau d'arco and Essiac, which is made from burdock root, Turkish rhubarb, slippery elm and sheep sorrel.

Wheatgrass juice, carrot juice, spirulina crystals and Klamath Lake blue-green algae increase the supply of oxygen in the blood.

Nutritional Supplements

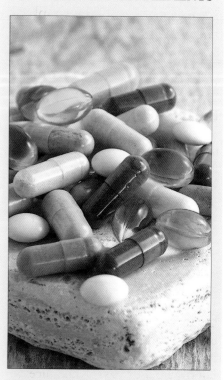

Although food is considered to be the best source of nutrients, the over-refining, processing and cooking of foods can destroy vital nutrients. Conventional cancer treatments can destroy many of the essential vitamins and nutrients found in the body, so people may benefit from taking additional nutritional supplements.

A recent report suggests that taking supplements is generally safe. However, it is recommended that you seek professional advice, particularly if you are taking anticoagulant medication or have high blood pressure.

Many nutritionists believe that antioxidants, including vitamin A, vitamin C, vitamin E, lutein, lycopene, beta-carotene and zeaxanthin, can help in the prevention and treatment of cancers. A study of people in 27 countries has also shown that the higher the blood selenium level, the lower the incidence of cancer.

JUICING

Freshly juiced vegetables, fruits, grasses and sprouts are an important element of a cancer prevention diet. They supply nutrients that the body may not get from cooked, processed foods and, because they are liquid, juices can be digested in minutes, compared with the hours it takes to digest foods with fibre. Fresh carrot is considered to be the most effective anti-cancer juice.

THE BENEFITS OF LIQUID FOODS

Juices that are taken as part of a health therapy are both nutritious and recuperative. It is important to use a wide variety of fruits and vegetables to obtain all the nutrients needed to combat illness and maintain health. Use organic fruits and vegetables, especially if cancer is already established. If these are not available, choose the freshest produce possible.

Enzymes from juices, which can be killed in cooking, work with the body's own enzymes, enabling better digestion and absorption, and nourishing the body. Drink juices as soon as they are made. Fresh juices from "live" ingredients contain oxygen and chlorophyll as well as vitamins, minerals and amino acids, which all help to rebuild and regenerate body tissues and cells.

An old-fashioned juicer can be used to squeeze the juice from citrus fruits.

Fresh fruit and vegetable juices are full of health-giving nutrients.

The Gerson diet is based on using organic fresh fruit and vegetable juices at regular intervals through the day. This process speeds detoxification and feeds the immune system. Fresh juices cleanse the body. They can also help to prevent constipation and encourage the healing of diverticulitis. Because energy is released so quickly, bringing juices into your diet can bring a joyful feeling that comes from eating live, vital foods.

WHAT TO JUICE

The nutritionist Dr Norman Walker, who lived to be over 100 years old, believed that the best anti-cancer juices were, firstly, fresh raw carrot juice and, secondly, carrot and spinach juice. The carrot juice molecule is exactly parallel to the human blood molecule. One pint or more of fresh carrot juice is recommended as a powerful cleanser and immune booster.

Celery, asparagus, watercress, parsley, kale, turnip and Swiss chard are also effective in cell regeneration and possess restorative healing properties. Some juices, such as beetroot, alfalfa and wheatgrass, can have a strong effect. Begin by sipping small amounts of the juice until you get used to it.

Fruits that are regarded as powerful anti-cancer agents are grapes and citrus fruits. Pear, peach, prune, watermelon, apple and papaya are also cleansing.

HOW TO JUICE

If you want to make therapeutic juices, you need to find a good juicer. You can extract the juice from citrus fruits by squeezing them, but many fruits and vegetables are hard and need a powerful juicer.

A blender is not suitable for making pure juices. Blended juices take much longer to digest because all the fibre is retained. A high-speed juicer leaves the cellulose and pulp behind. Wheatgrass requires a slow turning juicer because of its tough fibre.

High-speed electric juicers are either "centrifugal" or "masticating" juicers. Many nutritionists consider that one of the best juicers for extracting nutrients is the Champion juicer. It grinds the fruits and vegetables and squeezes them through firm meshing

Another type of juicer is a hydraulic press, which presses the plant fibres completely to squeeze out the juice. If you want to make fresh juices from wheatgrass or sprouts, you need to buy a fruit press, which is rather like an old-fashioned meat mincer.

If you incorporate regular juicing into your anti-cancer plan, it is worth investing in an efficient juicer, but any form of fresh organic juice is better than no juice at all. You can also chew wheatgrass, sprouts and fruits to extract their juice, and then spit out the fibre.

"LIVE" AND RAW FOODS

Cooking kills the enzymes in foods and also many of the vitamins, especially vitamin C, and delicate anti-cancer nutrients such as indoles can be destroyed in the cooking process. Including more raw and live foods in your diet means that you will absorb more enzymes, vitamins, minerals and antioxidants to keep you in good health. It is not a good idea to change suddenly to raw foods, as you may find them hard to digest if you are not used to them. Your taste buds may need educating, but you will be surprised to find that you soon develop a desire for the freshness of raw foods. Sprouted seeds, grains and legumes are an excellent source of living wholefoods.

"LIVE" FOODS

Sprouts are living anti-cancer foods – they are high in fibre and contain a rich supply of enzymes, vitamins, trace elements, chlorophyll and minerals such as calcium, potassium, phosphorous, iron and magnesium.

Almost any beans, seeds, or grains can be sprouted. It is important to use whole seeds that have not been treated with chemicals. Sesame seeds, aduki beans, mung beans, fenugreek and millet are all good for sprouting. Their flavours differ and the sprouts can sometimes be a little bitter, depending on how long they have been allowed to grow.

Some of the most nutritious and tasty sprouts can be grown from rye, almonds, chick-peas, pumpkin seeds, sesame seeds, sunflower seeds, lentils and mung beans. Mung and aduki bean sprouts are particularly good for transporting oxygen to cells. Sprouted beans and peas are less easy to digest than sprouted grains and seeds.

Live yogurt and sprouted seeds are powerful anti-cancer foods.

FERMENTED FOODS

Praised by many experts as powerful anti-cancer foods, fermented foods, such as "live" bio yogurt, buttermilk and soured cream, contain a bacteria *Lactobacillus acidophilus,* which is also present in the healthy, large intestine. When it is eaten in fermented foods, the small and large intestines are provided with healthy bacteria, and potentially harmful abnormal bacteria are prevented from forming.

Fermented foods are also rich in living enzymes, which encourage good digestion and absorption of nutrients.

As well as being rich in nutrients, yogurt is a predigested food, which makes it is easier for organs that have been weakened by ill health to digest.

Another fermented food, which is popularly used by centenarians in Russia and Bulgaria, is kefir. It is made by placing kefir grains in milk, then allowing the milk to coagulate.

SALADS

It is good to start a meal with a fresh vegetable salad, which acts as an internal cleanser. Grated and chopped carrots, cabbage, beetroot, celeriac, cucumber, watercress, celery, radishes, parsley, avocado, tomatoes and spring onions are all good salad ingredients.

Raw foods, especially fruits, should be chewed thoroughly. Eating them at the beginning of a meal, means they pass through the stomach quickly. Fresh fruits also help to dissolve toxic poisons and draw them through the system. Fresh citrus fruits, such as oranges, lemons, limes and grapefruit, contain over 50 anti-cancer agents.

Raw salad is a good internal cleanser.

HERBS

Many herbs are known and used for their medicinal properties, and some are thought to help prevent and treat cancer. Favourite herbs for cleansing and strengthening the system are thyme, parsley, basil, marjoram, tarragon and rosemary. The commonly found stinging nettle is also good for cleansing the blood. Milk thistle is a powerful herb for cleansing the liver, and turmeric, which contains circumin, has been recognized as protecting against cancer.

Astragalus is one of many Chinese herbs that can help to strengthen the immune system, and it is believed to be helpful for people fighting cancer. Fresh ginger is also popular for its anti-cancer properties. Herbalists believe that certain herbs can stop tumours growing and studies have shown that some herbs can be used to shrink tumours. Specialist advice should be sought if you plan to use herbs for medicinal purposes.

WHEATGRASS

Grown from the wholewheat grain, the healing properties of wheatgrass have been recognized for centuries. Wheatgrass juice is one of the best foods for helping to prevent and treat cancer. A powerful detoxifier, wheatgrass is high in enzymes, vitamins C and E, beta-carotene, minerals and phytochemicals. It also contains powerful anti-cancer agents including chlorophyll, abscisic acid, and B_{17}. Some nutritionists believe wheatgrass juice to be the best healing food available, especially for bolstering the immune system, cleansing the body, increasing oxygen and rejuvenating cells.

Wheatgrass

JUICING WHEATGRASS

A slow-turning juicer is needed for juicing wheatgrass because of its tough fibre. Keep wheatgrass juice in the fridge and use within a day.

Wheatgrass juice can be very powerful in its effect, and some people may feel dizzy or nauseous the first time they drink it. Begin by sipping small amounts until your body gets used to it.

Wheatgrass is usually grown to make juices rather than to be eaten because it is very fibrous and, in its whole form, is not easy to digest. If you don't have a juicer you can chew wheatgrass and spit out the pulp. However, it takes your body much longer to extract all the plant's vital nutrients in this way.

HOW TO SPROUT WHEATBERRIES

To sprout your own wheatgrass for making juice you will need:
• hard, organic wheatberries
• wide-mouthed glass jar
• nylon mesh or muslin
• 2 plastic trays, about 30 × 35cm/ 12 × 14in
• peat moss, compost or topsoil

3 Drain and rinse the berries. Cover the jar with muslin and leave the berries to sprout for 12 hours.

5 Water the seeds and cover with the other tray. After about 3 days, remove the top tray and place the tray of sprouting berries on a window ledge. Make sure you do not put them in direct sunlight as this may dry out the berries. Keep the berries moist, but not too wet.

6 Cut the wheatgrass when it is about 18cm/7in high. Try to cut the wheatgrass as close to the soil as possible, as this is where the greatest concentration of nutrients is found.

1 Fill a cup with wheatberries. Wash and rinse them thoroughly to remove any dirt.

2 Put the wheatberries in a jar, fill with water and leave them to soak overnight.

4 Put 2.5cm/1in of soil in one tray and scatter the seeds on top.

THE HEALTHY STORE CUPBOARD

When you are tired, ill or worried, you may find it difficult to remember which are the best foods to buy. You may find it helpful to keep a list of healthy foods in your kitchen cupboard, fridge or freezer. All the following foods have been found to have positive effects in preventing or treating cancer. Different foods possess different nutrients, but all help to boost the immune system.

SPICES AND SEASONINGS
Garlic
Miso
Pure soy sauce
Sea salt
Tamari
Turmeric
Umeboshi paste

Onions, garlic and ginger stimulate the body's antioxidant mechanisms.

Basil
Chives
Coriander
Ginger
Mint
Oregano
Rosemary
Sage
Tarragon
Thyme

GRAINS AND PULSES
Barley
Buckwheat
Bulgur wheat
Brown rice
Couscous
Millet
Muesli
Oats
Pasta
Sprouted grain breads
Wheat bran
Wholemeal breads

Organic muesli is high in fibre.

Black-eyed beans
Chick-peas
Lentils
Haricot beans
Kidney beans
Lima beans
Mung beans
Peas

COOKING AND PREPARATION TECHNIQUES
• Use steel cooking utensils; never use aluminium pans.
• Always wash fruit and vegetables to remove any dirt and contaminants. When cleaning vegetables, such as potatoes, turnips and carrots, use a scrubbing brush kept specifically for cleaning vegetables.
• Some fruits and vegetables, such as apples, cucumbers, lemons and aubergines have waxed skins – be sure to remove these before eating.
• Never eat meat that has been burned or charred in cooking.
• Remove all the skin from meat and poultry.

• Do not cook meat and fish in saturated or hydrogenated fats.
• Use extra virgin olive oil for cooking and salad dressings.
• Do not add extra salt to foods when eating your meals.
• Boil, steam, stir-fry and bake foods whenever possible. These are considered to be effective and healthy ways of preparing foods, and ensure the foods are easy to digest.
• When you prepare a meal, think of it as creating a painting. Foods that are pleasing to the eye can stimulate the digestive juices. Try to balance textures and colours, using herbs as sprigs of colour – they will also exude an enticing aroma.

• Experiment with health-giving herbs to give flavour to foods that may seem bland, especially in the early days of trying a low-fat diet.

Use herbs to add flavour, colour and texture to a dish.

NUTS AND SEEDS

Almonds
Brazil nuts
Nut butters
Pecan nuts
Pine nuts
Poppy seeds
Pumpkin seeds
Sesame seeds
Sunflower seeds
Walnuts

Nut butters have anti-cancer properties.

PACKAGED FOODS

Dried unsulphured fruits, such as dates, raisins, sultanas, apricots and prunes
Extra virgin olive oil
Honey
Hummus
Klamath Lake blue-green algae
Linseed oil
Liquorice
Oily fish, such as mackerel, salmon, sardines, tuna, herring and eel
Rapeseed oil (canola)
Sauerkraut
Seaweeds, such as nori, laver, arame, wakami, kelp and kombu
Spirulina
Tahini
Tofu
Tempeh
Whole apple cider vinegar

Dried fruits are a useful source of energy and are packed with vitamins and nutrients, including vitamin C, beta-carotene, potassium and iron.

FRUIT

Apples
Apricots
Bananas
Blueberries
Blackberries
Blackcurrants
Canteloupe melons
Cherries
Figs
Red grapes
Gooseberries
Grapefruit
Grapes
Kiwi fruits
Lemons
Limes
Peaches
Pineapples
Mangoes
Nectarines
Oranges
Raspberries
Red grapes
Redcurrants
Strawberries
Watermelons
White currants

VEGETABLES

Asparagus
Aubergines
Avocados
Beetroot
Broccoli
Broad beans
Brussels sprouts
Cabbages
Carrots
Cauliflowers
Celery
Kale
Onions
Parsnips
Potatoes
Pumpkins
Shiitake mushrooms
Spinach
Squash
Swedes
Sweet potatoes (yams)
Red, orange, yellow and green peppers
Tomatoes
Turnips

Dark green vegetables are rich in folates and contain vitamin E, which strengthens the immune system.

DAIRY FOODS

"Live" yogurt
Low-fat cheeses, such as quark, ricotta
  and cottage cheese
Organic low-fat milk

*Buttermilk, soured cream and yogurt are
rich in valuable enzymes and healthy
bacteria, which aid the digestion.*

FISH, POULTRY AND EGGS

Fresh oily fish, such as mackerel,
  sardines, trout, salmon, tuna and eel
Organic chicken and turkey
Fresh, organic, free-range eggs

*Eat plenty of oily fish, such as tuna and
salmon, obtained from clean salt or fresh
water sources.*

BEVERAGES

Green, black and ginseng tea
Mineral water (low sodium)
Pure fruit and vegetable juices
Good red wine, preferably organic

*Black tea, green tea and ginseng tea help
cleanse the blood and and increase the
supply of oxygen.*

CHOOSING ORGANIC

Unfortunately, most foods are still
grown with the use of agrochemicals,
including synthetic fertilizers, growth
promoters and pesticides. Studies
show that these chemicals in foods
can be deposited in fatty body tissue,
where they can be harmful to health.
All too often, as a result of these
farming methods, the soil is depleted
of selenium, which is known to be a
vital and powerful antioxidant that
helps to prevent and treat cancer.

The arguments for choosing to eat
organic products are powerful. Fruits
and vegetables have a fuller, fresher
flavour. It is also reassuring to know
that they are unadulterated and
completely natural, and haven't been
waxed or gassed.

Organic meat is produced from
free-range, grass-fed animals, which
have not been given antibiotics,
hormones, growth-promoters or feed
additives. If you choose to eat organic
meats and poultry, you will also have
the satisfaction of knowing that the
animals lived and died humanely.

Organic free-range eggs are
produced from hens that are fed on a
natural pesticide-free diet, which has
not had hormones or artificial
colourants added. The hens are able
to roam on land that has not been
treated with chemical fertilizers and
is certified organic.

Organic products often have a
better flavour and have no added
chemicals, sugar or salt. Always
check the labels carefully to ensure
that products really are organic.

Many supermarkets are responding
to public demand for organic foods.
If you would like a greater variety of
organic foods, make it known to
your local food store – the greater
the demand, the more likely your
store will be to stock these products,
and the lower the price.

*Organic free-range eggs contain the
valuable antioxidant, vitamin A and
are high in protein.*

A HEALTHIER LIFESTYLE

Even the circumstances under which you eat your meals are important, not only in terms of your enjoyment but also in the way in which it affects your ability to digest food and to assimilate nutrients. You may find it hard to relax and to maintain inner calm in today's hectic world. If you can change any harmful living and eating patterns, you may lessen your chances of getting cancer. You can try to protect your life energy by exercising, practising relaxation and meditation. It is good to think positively, and it is important to recognize strong feelings like anger, fear and sadness and find a safe way to express them. Feeling out of control can depress your immune system.

HARMONIOUS EATING

It is easier to digest food if you eat in a peaceful environment, when you are calm and not stressed. Life is often such a rush that it seems difficult to prepare food with pleasure, gratitude and love. Concentrate fully on your meal rather than watching television or talking too much and gulping in air.

A beautiful table setting will enhance your enjoyment of a meal.

Cultivate your enjoyment of pure, simple foods and do not eat more than you need. Even if you are eating alone, make your table beautiful with a candle or a flower and give yourself the best you can, not only in foods but in creating a harmonious environment.

COMPLEMENTARY THERAPIES

Rather than concentrating on the body alone, complementary medicine offers many therapies that support the person as a whole, and has proved to be effective in treating cancer.

Counselling can provide a safe and non-judgemental environment where you can talk about your often painful thoughts, feelings and experiences and be listened to and supported.

Naturopathy offers guidance on diet, fasting, exercises and hydrotherapy to naturally restore the body to health.

Aromatherapy uses aromatic essences with therapeutic qualities to massage the body. This relaxes the muscles and gives a greater sense of well-being.

Reflexology is a form of massage based on the belief that different areas of the feet relate to parts of the body.

Homeopathy uses minute amounts of natural remedies to stimulate the body's own healing powers.

Traditional Chinese medicine offers herbal treatments, acupuncture and acupressure. Using needles or massage techniques, the energy points in the body are stimulated to create or restore balance, harmony and health.

Herbal medicine uses whole plants as remedies and concentrates on the health of the whole person.

Creative visualization requires you to visualize cancer cells being zapped and dying, and the immune system creating healthy cells and tissue.

In spiritual healing, the healer's hands are gently laid on you or held near you. The body is made well through visualization and prayer.

Yoga offers a simpler approach to living with proper exercise, breathing, relaxing, eating and with positive thinking and meditation.

Oriental forms of exercise have been shown to be good for dealing with cancer. In the East millions of people rise at dawn to practise tai chi, which is seen as essential therapy for health and a long life.

Do-In is a Japanese form of self-massage, which stimulates the body's acupressure points and increases the flow of energy in the body.

RELAXATION AND MEDITATION

Create your own sanctuary of inner peace. Find a comfortable spot in quiet surroundings and choose a regular time to sit there quietly each day for at least ten minutes. Listen to your breathing and still your mind of restless thoughts. It may help to calm your thoughts by playing some soothing music.

Imagine your body being filled with peaceful, white light that washes away your worries and pains. Concentrate on relaxing your muscles in turn, from toes to head. Return to this calm place inside yourself whenever you need to.

Help to eliminate toxins from the body and bring greater vitality and inner peace through relaxation and meditation.

SOUPS AND STARTERS

On cold winter days, start your meal with a warming soup.

The hot soups included here – Creamed Spinach and Potato Soup,

Potato and Garlic Broth, and Farmhouse Soup served with

wholemeal bread – are filling enough to make a meal on their own.

In summer, enjoy the Mediterranean flavours of Gazpacho with

Avocado Salsa or Marinated Baby Aubergines; or try a Turkish-style

mezze with Sesame Seed-coated Falafel or Hummus.

Creamed Spinach and Potato Soup

Spinach fills this low-fat, creamy soup with antioxidant nutrients.

Ingredients

Serves 6
1 large onion, finely chopped
1 garlic clove, crushed
900g/2lb floury potatoes, diced
2 celery sticks, chopped
1.2 litres/2 pints/5 cups basic
   vegetable stock
250g/9oz fresh spinach leaves
200g/7oz/scant 1 cup low-fat
   cream cheese
300ml/½ pint/1¼ cups milk
dash of dry sherry
salt and freshly ground black pepper
croûtons and chopped fresh parsley,
   to garnish

1 Place the onion, garlic, potatoes and celery in a large saucepan. Add the stock and simmer for 20 minutes.

2 Season the soup, add the spinach, then cook for a further 10 minutes. Remove from the heat and leave to cool slightly.

3 Process the soup in batches and return to the saucepan. Stir in the cream cheese and milk, then simmer gently until warmed through. Check the seasoning and add a dash of sherry. Serve garnished with croûtons and chopped parsley.

NUTRITION NOTES

Per portion:

Energy	132kcals/561kJ
Protein	3.6g
Fat	0.2g
Saturated fat	0g
Carbohydrate	30.7g
Fibre	2.3g
Sugars	1.5g
Calcium	10mg

Potato and Garlic Broth

A perfect winter warmer, this wholesome soup is packed with phytochemical-rich garlic, which is believed to help in the fight against cancer.

Ingredients

Serves 6
2 whole heads of garlic
4 potatoes, peeled and diced
1.75 litres/3 pints/7½ cups basic
   vegetable stock
salt and freshly ground black pepper
flat leaf parsley, to garnish

HEALTH BENEFITS

The American National Cancer Institute rates garlic as one of the top foods for cancer prevention. It is best eaten raw, but cooking does not greatly reduce its beneficial qualities.

1 Preheat the oven to 190°C/375°F/ Gas 5. Place the unpeeled garlic bulbs in a small roasting tin and bake for 30 minutes.

2 Meanwhile, par-cook the potatoes in boiling water for 10 minutes.

3 Simmer the prepared vegetable stock for 5 minutes. Drain the potatoes and add to the stock.

4 Squeeze the garlic pulp into the soup, stir and season to taste.

5 Simmer for a further 15 minutes and then pour into warmed bowls and garnish with flat leaf parsley.

COOK'S TIP

Too much garlic can be overpowering, but roasting it first mellows its pungent flavour.

NUTRITION NOTES

Per portion:

Energy	290kcals/1225kJ
Protein	16.1g
Fat	4.2g
Saturated fat	2.0g
Carbohydrate	46.3g
Fibre	4.6g
Sugars	8.4g
Calcium	253mg

Italian Farmhouse Soup

Ingredients

Serves 4

30ml/2 tbsp olive oil
1 onion, roughly chopped
3 carrots, cut into large chunks
200g/7oz turnips, cut into large chunks
175g/6oz swede, cut into large chunks
400g/14oz can chopped tomatoes
15ml/1 tbsp tomato purée
5ml/1 tsp dried mixed herbs
5ml/1 tsp dried oregano
50g/2oz/½ cup dried peppers, washed
  and thinly sliced (optional)
1.5 litres/2½ pints/6¼ cups vegetable
  stock or water
50g/2oz/½ cup dried small macaroni
  or conchiglie
400g/14oz can red kidney beans, rinsed
  and drained
30ml/2 tbsp chopped fresh flat
  leaf parsley
salt and freshly ground black pepper
freshly grated Parmesan cheese, to serve

1 Heat the oil in a large saucepan, add the onion and cook over a low heat for about 5 minutes until softened. Add the fresh vegetables, canned tomatoes, tomato purée, dried herbs and dried peppers, if using. Stir in salt and pepper to taste.

2 Pour in the stock or water and bring to the boil. Stir well, cover, lower the heat and simmer for 30 minutes, stirring occasionally.

3 Add the pasta and bring to the boil, stirring. Lower the heat and simmer, uncovered, until the pasta is only just *al dente*: about 5 minutes or according to the instructions on the packet. Stir frequently.

4 Stir in the beans. Heat through for 2–3 minutes, then remove from the heat and stir in the parsley. Taste the soup for seasoning. Serve hot with grated Parmesan handed separately.

Nutrition Notes

Per portion:

Energy	248kcals/1049kJ
Protein	10.3g
Fat	6.7g
Saturated fat	0.9g
Carbohydrate	39g
Fibre	10.5g
Sugars	12.8g
Calcium	143mg

Cook's Tip

Packets of dried Italian peppers are piquant and firm with a "meaty" bite to them, which makes them ideal for adding substance to vegetarian soups.

Variation

Root vegetables form the base of this soup, but you can vary the vegetables according to what you have to hand.

Gazpacho with Avocado Salsa

This classic summer soup, which is loaded with fresh vegetables, chilli and garlic, does not require cooking. Heat can often destroy valuable nutrients, so this soup makes a perfect choice.

INGREDIENTS

Serves 4

2 slices day-old bread
600ml/1 pint/2½ cups chilled water
1kg/2¼lb large vine-ripened tomatoes
1 medium cucumber
1 red pepper, seeded and chopped
1 green chilli, seeded and chopped
2 garlic cloves, chopped
30ml/2 tbsp olive oil
juice of 1 lime and 1 lemon
a few drops of Tabasco
salt and freshly ground black pepper
8 ice cubes, to serve
a handful of basil leaves, to garnish

For the croûtons
2 slices day-old bread, crusts removed
1 garlic clove
15ml/1 tbsp olive oil

For the avocado salsa
1 ripe avocado, stoned, peeled
  and diced
5ml/1 tsp lemon juice
2.5cm/1in piece cucumber, diced
½ red chilli, finely chopped

1 Soak the bread in 150ml/¼ pint/⅔ cup of the water for 5 minutes.

NUTRITION NOTES

Per portion:

Energy	199kcals/836kJ
Protein	5.4g
Fat	10.0g
Saturated fat	2.4g
Carbohydrate	23.3g
Fibre	5.8g
Sugars	12.1g
Calcium	59mg

2 Meanwhile, pour boiling water over the tomatoes and leave for 30 seconds–1 minute, then peel, seed and chop the flesh. Peel the cucumber and cut in half lengthways. Scoop out the seeds with a spoon, discard, and chop the flesh into small cubes.

3 Place the bread, tomatoes, chopped cucumber, red pepper, chilli, garlic, olive oil, citrus juices and Tabasco in a food processor or blender with the remaining chilled water and blend until well combined but still chunky. Season to taste and chill for 2–3 hours.

4 To make the croûtons, rub the slices of bread with the garlic clove. Cut into cubes, place in a plastic bag with the olive oil, and shake until coated with the oil. Fry the croûtons until crisp and golden.

5 To make the avocado salsa, toss the avocado in the lemon juice and combine with the cucumber and chilli.

6 Ladle the soup into bowls, add the ice cubes, and top with a spoonful of salsa and croûtons. Garnish with basil just before serving.

Sesame Seed-coated Falafel with Tahini Yogurt Dip

Sesame seeds make a nutritious coating for these spicy patties.

INGREDIENTS

Serves 4
250g/9oz/2⅔ cups dried chick-peas
2 garlic cloves, crushed
1 red chilli, seeded and finely sliced
5ml/1 tsp ground coriander
5ml/1 tsp ground cumin
15ml/1 tbsp chopped fresh mint
15ml/1 tbsp chopped fresh parsley
2 spring onions, finely chopped
1 large egg, beaten
sesame seeds, for coating
sunflower oil, for frying
salt and freshly ground black pepper
pitta bread, to serve

For the tahini yogurt dip
200g/7oz/2⅓ cups natural yogurt
30ml/2 tbsp light tahini
5ml/1 tsp cayenne pepper, plus extra
   for sprinkling
15ml/1 tbsp chopped fresh mint
1 spring onion, finely sliced

1 Soak the chick-peas overnight in cold water. Drain and rinse the chick-peas, then place in a saucepan and cover with cold water. Bring to the boil and boil for 10 minutes, then reduce the heat and simmer for about 1½ hours until tender. Drain.

2 Meanwhile, make the dip. Place the yogurt, tahini, cayenne and chopped mint in a bowl and mix well. Sprinkle with the sliced spring onion and extra cayenne pepper. Chill in the fridge until required.

3 Combine the chick-peas with the garlic, chilli, ground spices, fresh herbs, spring onions and seasoning, then mix with the egg. Place in a food processor and blend until the mixture forms a coarse paste. If the paste seems too soft, leave it to chill for 30 minutes.

4 Form the chilled chick-pea paste into 12 patties with your hands, then roll each one in the sesame seeds.

5 Heat enough oil in a large frying pan to shallow fry the falafel. Fry for 6 minutes, turning once – you may need to do this in batches.

6 Serve with a spoonful of the yogurt dip and warm pitta bread.

NUTRITION NOTES	
Per portion:	
Energy	348kcals/1458kJ
Protein	19.3g
Fat	15.4g
Saturated fat	2.5g
Carbohydrate	35.0g
Fibre	7.4g
Sugars	5.7g
Calcium	258mg

— HEALTH BENEFITS —

Chick-peas contain lignins, also known as phytoestrogens, which are thought to protect against certain cancers. Sesame seeds are rich in the antioxidant vitamin E.

Hummus

Blending chick-peas with garlic and olive oil makes a delicious dip or healthy sandwich filler. This creamy purée contains fibre, plant protein and antioxidants – all of which are important in the fight against cancer.

INGREDIENTS

Serves 6
150g/5oz/¾ cup dried chick-peas
juice of 2 lemons
2 garlic cloves, sliced
30ml/2 tbsp olive oil
pinch of cayenne pepper
150ml/¼ pint/⅔ cup tahini paste
extra olive oil and cayenne pepper
  for sprinkling
salt and freshly ground black pepper
black olives, to serve

1 Put the chick-peas in a bowl with plenty of cold water and leave to soak overnight.

2 Drain the chick-peas and cover with fresh water in a saucepan. Bring to the boil and boil rapidly for 10 minutes. Reduce the heat and simmer gently for about 1½–2 hours until soft. Drain.

3 Process the chick-peas in a food processor or blender, to a smooth purée. Add the lemon juice, garlic, olive oil, cayenne pepper and tahini and blend until creamy, from time to time scraping the mixture down from the sides of the bowl.

4 Season the purée with salt and pepper and transfer to a serving dish. Sprinkle with oil and cayenne pepper and serve with olives.

COOK'S TIP

For convenience, canned chick-peas can be used instead. Allow two 400g/14oz cans and drain them thoroughly. Tahini paste can be purchased from most supermarkets and health food shops.

NUTRITION NOTES

Per portion:

Energy	281kcals/1169kJ
Protein	9.9g
Fat	21.6g
Saturated fat	3.0g
Carbohydrate	12.7g
Fibre	4.6g
Sugars	0.8g
Calcium	210mg

Layered Vegetable Terrine

This layered combination of fresh vegetables and herbs is baked in the oven – a healthy and effective way of cooking foods.

INGREDIENTS

Serves 6

3 red peppers, halved
450g/1lb potatoes
115g/4oz spinach leaves, trimmed
25g/1oz/2 tbsp butter
pinch grated nutmeg
115g/4oz vegetarian Cheddar cheese, grated
1 courgette, sliced lengthways and blanched
salt and freshly ground black pepper

COOK'S TIP

Get all of the ingredients prepared before you start the layering process, to make sure that you don't forget anything.

1 Preheat the oven to 180°C/350°F/Gas 4. Place the peppers in a roasting tin and roast them with the cores in place for 30–45 minutes until charred. Remove from the oven. Place in plastic bag to cool. Peel the skins and remove the cores. Peel the potatoes and boil in plenty of salted water for 10–15 minutes until tender.

2 Blanch the spinach for a few seconds in boiling water. Drain and pat dry on kitchen paper.

3 Line the base and sides of a 900g/2lb loaf tin, making sure the leaves overlap slightly.

4 Slice the potatoes thinly and lay one-third of the potatoes over the base, dot with a little of the butter and season with salt, pepper and nutmeg. Sprinkle a little cheese over.

5 Arrange three of the peeled pepper halves on top. Sprinkle a little cheese over and then a layer of courgettes. Lay another one-third of the potatoes on top with the remaining peppers and some more cheese, seasoning as you go. Lay the final layer of potato on top and scatter over any remaining cheese. Fold the spinach leaves over. Cover with foil.

6 Place the loaf tin in a roasting tin and pour boiling water around the outside, making sure the water comes halfway up the sides of the tin. Bake for 45 minutes–1 hour, until soft. Remove from the oven and turn the loaf out. Serve sliced.

NUTRITION NOTES

Per portion:

Energy	155kcals/684kJ
Protein	7.7g
Fat	7.5g
Saturated fat	4.5g
Carbohydrate	17.1g
Fibre	2.4g
Sugars	5.7g
Calcium	179mg

Marinated Baby Aubergines

This recipe has a strong Italian influence and uses traditional Mediterranean ingredients. These are high in antioxidants and have been shown to lower the incidence of cancer.

INGREDIENTS

Serves 4

12 baby aubergines, halved lengthways
250ml/8fl oz/1 cup extra virgin
   olive oil
juice of 1 lemon
30ml/2 tbsp balsamic vinegar
3 cloves
25g/1oz/⅓ cup pine nuts
25g/1oz/2 tbsp raisins
15ml/1 tbsp sugar
1 bay leaf
large pinch of dried chilli flakes
salt and freshly ground black pepper

1 Preheat the grill to high. Place the aubergines, cut side up, in the grill pan and brush with a little of the olive oil. Grill for 10 minutes, until golden brown, turning them over halfway through cooking.

NUTRITION NOTES

Per portion:

Energy	507kcals/2095kJ
Protein	2.7g
Fat	50.6g
Saturated fat	6.9g
Carbohydrate	11.6g
Fibre	3.2g
Sugars	11.3g
Calcium	20mg

HEALTH BENEFITS

Aubergines contain bioflavonoids, which are thought to reduce the risk of certain types of cancer. Olive oil and pine nuts are rich sources of the antioxidant vitamin E, which can help fight off free radicals that have the potential to cause cancer.

2 To make the marinade, put the remaining olive oil, the lemon juice, vinegar, cloves, pine nuts, raisins, sugar and bay leaf in a jug. Add the chilli flakes, season with salt and pepper and mix well.

3 Place the hot aubergines in an earthenware or glass bowl, and pour over the marinade. Leave to cool, turning the aubergines once or twice. Serve cold.

FISH DISHES

Fish is a very nutritious food, an excellent source of complete protein, iron and other minerals. Oily fish such as sardines and mackerel are rich in health-giving omega-3 fatty acids. Try these delicious fish recipes from all over the world – Baked Fish with Tahini Sauce from North Africa, traditional Coconut Fish with Rice Noodles from Burma, Sardine Gratin from the Mediterranean, or Salmon cooked in the Scandinavian style, but transformed with Thai spices.

Fish Pie with Sweet Potato Topping

INGREDIENTS

Serves 6

175g/6oz/1 cup basmati rice, soaked
450ml/¾ pint/scant 2 cups
    well-flavoured stock
175g/6oz broad beans
675g/1½lb skinned haddock or
    cod fillets
about 450ml/¾ pint/scant 2 cups milk
40g/1½oz/3 tbsp butter
30–45ml/2–3 tbsp plain flour
15ml/1 tbsp chopped fresh parsley
salt and freshly ground black pepper
sugar snap peas, to serve

For the topping
450g/1lb sweet potatoes
450g/1lb floury white potatoes, such as
    King Edwards
butter and milk, for mashing
15ml/1 tbsp single cream (optional)
10ml/2 tsp chopped fresh parsley
5ml/1 tsp chopped fresh dill

1 Preheat the oven to 190°C/375°F/
Gas 5. Drain the rice and then
cook in the lightly salted stock in a
covered pan for about 10 minutes
or according to the instructions on
the packet.

2 Cook the broad beans in lightly
salted water until tender and drain.
When cool enough to handle, skin the
beans, discarding the outer skin.

3 To make the topping, cook the
sweet and white potatoes separately
in boiling salted water. Mash them
both with a little milk and butter,
adding the cream, if using. Add the
parsley and dill to the sweet potatoes.

4 Place the fish fillets in a shallow pan
and add about 350ml/12fl oz/
1½ cups of the milk or enough to just
cover the fish. Dot with 15ml/1 tbsp
of the butter and season with salt and
pepper. Heat gently and then simmer
for about 6 minutes until the fish is
just tender.

5 Break the fish into large pieces.
Then pour the cooking liquid into
a measuring jug and make up to
450ml/¾ pint/scant 2 cups with the
remaining milk.

6 Make a white sauce. Melt the
remaining butter in a saucepan and
stir in the flour. Add the milk from the
fish and cook, stirring, to make a fairly
thin white sauce. Stir in the parsley
and season.

7 Place the cooked rice at the
bottom of a casserole. Add the
broad beans and fish on top and pour
over the white sauce. Spoon the
mashed potatoes over the top to make
an attractive pattern. Dot with a little
extra butter and bake for 15 minutes
until lightly browned. Serve with sugar
snap peas.

NUTRITION NOTES	
Per portion:	
Energy	663kcals/2695kJ
Protein	39g
Fat	15.9g
Saturated fat	9.4g
Carbohydrate	88.1g
Fibre	7.1g
Sugars	8.7g
Calcium	100mg

Sardine Gratin

Sardines are an excellent choice of fish because they contain high levels of omega-3 fatty acids, which play a key role in cancer prevention and intervention.

INGREDIENTS

Serves 4

15ml/1 tbsp light olive oil
½ small onion, finely chopped
2 garlic cloves, crushed
40g/1½oz/6 tbsp blanched
   almonds, chopped
25g/1oz/2 tbsp sultanas,
   roughly chopped
10 pitted black olives, chopped
30ml/2 tbsp capers, roughly chopped
30ml/2 tbsp roughly chopped
   fresh parsley
50g/2oz/1 cup breadcrumbs
16 large sardines, scaled and gutted
25g/1oz/⅓ cup freshly grated
   Parmesan cheese
salt and freshly ground black pepper
flat leaf parsley, to garnish

1 Preheat the oven to 200°C/400°F/ Gas 6. Lightly oil a large, shallow ovenproof dish.

NUTRITION NOTES

Per portion:

Energy	450kcals/1886kJ
Protein	39.3g
Fat	26.3g
Saturated fat	6.6g
Carbohydrate	15.3g
Fibre	1.5g
Sugars	5.5g
Calcium	260mg

HEALTH BENEFITS

Oily fish such as sardines are rich in omega-3 essential fatty acids – a key element in cancer prevention. Almonds contain the antioxidant vitamin E, which is associated with a lower risk of cancer.

2 Heat the oil in a frying pan and fry the onion and garlic gently for 3 minutes. Stir in the almonds, sultanas, olives, capers, parsley and 25g/1oz/ ½ cup of the breadcrumbs. Season lightly with salt and pepper.

3 Make 2–3 diagonal cuts on each side of the sardines. Fill the cavities with stuffing and lay the sardines in the prepared dish.

4 Mix the remaining breadcrumbs with the cheese and scatter over the fish. Bake for about 20 minutes until the fish is cooked through. Test by piercing one sardine through the thickest part with a knife.

5 Garnish with parsley and serve immediately with a leafy salad.

Spiced Fish with Pumpkin Rice

This North African dish is a contrast of mild spicy fish and slightly sweet pumpkin. This orange-fleshed vegetable is a good source of the powerful antioxidant, beta-carotene, which boosts the immune system, provides oxygen to the cells and helps the body to fight cancer.

INGREDIENTS

Serves 4
450g/1lb sea bass or other firm fish
30ml/2 tbsp plain flour
5ml/1 tsp ground coriander
1.5–2.5ml/¼–½ tsp ground turmeric
about 500g/1¼lb piece of pumpkin
30–45ml/2–3 tbsp olive oil
about 6 spring onions,
    sliced diagonally
1 garlic clove, finely chopped
275g/10oz/1½ cups basmati
    rice, soaked
550ml/18fl oz/2½ cups fish stock
salt and freshly ground black pepper
lime or lemon wedges and fresh
    coriander sprigs, to garnish

For the coriander and ginger flavouring mixture
45ml/3 tbsp finely chopped
    fresh coriander
10ml/2 tsp finely chopped fresh
    root ginger
½–1 fresh chilli, seeded and very
    finely chopped
45ml/3 tbsp lime or lemon juice

— NUTRITION NOTES —	
Per portion:	
Energy	479kcals/2004kJ
Protein	28.7g
Fat	11.8g
Saturated fat	1.8g
Carbohydrate	63.9g
Fibre	1.7g
Sugars	2.7g
Calcium	212mg

1 Carefully remove and discard any skin or bones from the fish and cut into 2cm/¾in chunks. Mix together the flour, coriander, turmeric and a little salt and pepper in a plastic bag. Then add the chunks of fish and shake for a few seconds so that each piece is evenly coated in the spice mixture. Set aside.

2 Make the coriander and ginger flavouring mixture by stirring the ingredients together in a small bowl.

3 Cut the skin from the pumpkin with a sharp knife and scoop out the seeds. Then cut the flesh into 2cm/¾in chunks.

4 Heat 15ml/1 tbsp of the oil in a wok or flameproof casserole and stir-fry the spring onions and garlic for a few minutes until slightly softened and golden. Add the pumpkin and cook over a fairly low heat, stirring frequently, for 4–5 minutes or until the flesh softens.

5 Drain the rice, add to the wok or casserole and stir-fry over a brisk heat for 2–3 minutes. Then stir in the stock together with a little salt. Bring to simmering point, then cover and cook over a low heat for about 15 minutes until the rice and pumpkin are tender.

6 About 4 minutes before the rice is ready, heat the remaining oil in a frying pan and fry the fish over a moderately high heat for 3 minutes until the outside is lightly browned and crisp and the flesh is cooked through but still moist.

7 Just before serving, carefully stir the coriander and ginger flavouring mixture into the rice and transfer to a warmed serving dish. Lay the fish pieces on top of the rice or, alternatively, stir into the rice. Serve garnished with lime or lemon wedges and sprigs of fresh coriander.

Baked Fish with Tahini Sauce

INGREDIENTS

Serves 4

1 whole fish, about 1.2kg/2½lb, scaled
   and cleaned
10ml/2 tsp coriander seeds
4 garlic cloves, sliced
10ml/2 tsp harissa sauce
90ml/6 tbsp olive oil
6 plum tomatoes, sliced
1 mild onion, sliced
3 preserved lemons or 1 fresh lemon
salt and freshly ground black pepper
plenty of fresh herbs, such as bay leaves,
   thyme and rosemary

For the sauce

75ml/3fl oz/⅓ cup light tahini
juice of 1 lemon
1 garlic clove, crushed
45ml/3 tbsp finely chopped fresh
   parsley or coriander
extra herbs, to garnish

1 Preheat the oven to 200°C/400°F/ Gas 6. Grease the base and sides of a large, shallow ovenproof dish or roasting tin.

2 Slash the fish diagonally on both sides with a sharp knife. Finely crush the coriander seeds and garlic with a pestle and mortar. Mix with the harissa sauce and about 60ml/4 tbsp of the olive oil.

3 Spread a little of the coriander, garlic and harissa paste inside the cavity of the fish. Spread the remainder over each side of the fish and set aside.

4 Scatter the tomatoes, onion and preserved or fresh lemon into the dish. (Thinly slice the lemon if using fresh.) Sprinkle with the remaining oil and season with salt and pepper. Lay the fish on top and tuck plenty of herbs around it.

5 Bake, uncovered, for about 25 minutes, or until the fish has turned opaque – test by piercing the thickest part with a knife.

6 Meanwhile, make the sauce. Mix the tahini, lemon juice, garlic and parsley or coriander in a small saucepan with 120ml/4fl oz/½ cup water and add a little salt and pepper. Cook gently until smooth and heated through. Serve with the fish.

NUTRITION NOTES	
Per portion:	
Energy	481kcals/2002kJ
Protein	46g
Fat	31.1g
Saturated fat	4.6g
Carbohydrate	4.2g
Fibre	2.6g
Sugars	3.8g
Calcium	187mg

Coconut Fish with Rice Noodles

This spicy dish from Burma is the ideal way to introduce more oily fish, and all its valuable nutrients, into your diet. Some experts recommend eating oily fish, such as mackerel, two or three times a week.

INGREDIENTS

Serves 8

675g/1½lb huss, cod or mackerel, cleaned but left on the bone
3 lemon grass stalks
2.5cm/1in piece fresh root ginger, peeled
30ml/2 tbsp fish sauce
3 onions, roughly chopped
4 garlic cloves, roughly chopped
2–3 fresh red chillies, seeded and chopped
5ml/1 tsp ground turmeric
75ml/5 tbsp groundnut oil, for frying
400ml/14fl oz/1⅔ cups canned coconut milk
45ml/3 tbsp rice flour
45ml/3 tbsp chick-pea flour (besan)
500g/1½lb drained canned bamboo shoot, cut into chunks
salt and freshly ground black pepper

To serve
450g/1lb dried or fresh rice noodles, cooked according to the instructions on the packet
wedges of hard-boiled egg; thinly sliced onions; chopped spring onions and fried prawns and chillies

---
NUTRITION NOTES

Per portion:

Energy	497kcals/2073kJ
Protein	20.8g
Fat	21.0g
Saturated fat	4.3g
Carbohydrate	109.2g
Fibre	3.7g
Sugars	8.5g
Calcium	102.5mg

1 Place the fish in a large pan and pour in cold water to cover. Bruise two lemon grass stalks and half the ginger and add to the pan. Bring to the boil, add the fish sauce and cook for 10 minutes.

2 Lift out the fish and allow to cool while straining the stock into a large bowl. Discard the skin and bones from the fish and reserve the flesh, which will be in small pieces.

3 Cut off the lower 5cm/2in of the remaining lemon grass stalk and chop it roughly. Put it in a food processor or blender along with the remaining ginger, the onions, garlic, chillies and turmeric.

4 Process to a smooth paste. Heat the oil in a frying pan and fry the paste until it gives off a rich aroma. Remove from the heat and add the fish.

5 Stir the coconut milk into the reserved fish stock. Add enough water to make up to 2.4 litres/4 pints/10 cups and pour into a large pan. In a jug, mix the rice and chick-pea (besan) flours to a thin cream with some of the stock. Stir this into the coconut and stock mixture and bring to the boil, stirring all the time.

6 Add the bamboo shoots and cook for about 10 minutes until just tender. Stir in the fish. Check the seasoning, cover and heat through. Guests pour soup over the noodles and choose their own accompaniments.

Baked Trout with Rice and Sun-dried Tomatoes

Trout, with its rich supply of omega-3 fatty acids and other cancer-fighting nutrients, is always a healthy choice.

INGREDIENTS

Serves 4

2 fresh, filleted trout, each about
  500g/1¼lb unfilleted weight
75g/3oz/½ cup mixed unsalted
  cashews, pine nuts, almonds
  or hazelnuts
25ml/1½ tbsp olive oil, plus extra
  for cooking
1 small onion, finely chopped
10ml/2 tsp grated fresh root ginger
175g/6oz/1 cup cooked long grain rice
4 tomatoes, peeled and finely chopped
4 sun-dried tomatoes, chopped
30ml/2 tbsp chopped fresh tarragon
salt and freshly ground black pepper
salad leaves, to garnish

1 Ask your fishmonger to fillet the trout, or use a sharp knife and cut away the bones, leaving as little flesh on the bones as possible. Check for any tiny bones and remove using tweezers.

2 Preheat the oven to 190°C/375°F/ Gas 5. Put the nuts in a shallow baking tin and bake in the oven for 3–4 minutes until golden, shaking the tin occasionally. Chop roughly.

3 Heat the oil in a small frying pan and fry the onion for 3–4 minutes until soft and golden. Stir in the ginger and cook for another minute and spoon into a mixing bowl. Stir in the rice, tomatoes, sun-dried tomatoes, toasted nuts and tarragon, and season with salt and pepper.

4 Place the two trout on pieces of oiled foil and spoon the stuffing into the filleted cavities. Bring the foil round to encircle each fish and add a sprig of tarragon and a drizzle of olive oil to each.

5 Fold the foil over to secure and place the fish parcels in a large roasting tin. Cook in the oven for 20–25 minutes until the fish is just tender – test with a knife.

6 Cut the fish into thick slices and serve, garnished with salad leaves.

--- NUTRITION NOTES ---

Per portion:

Energy	726kcals/3045kJ
Protein	55.7g
Fat	38.7g
Saturated fat	7.8g
Carbohydrate	41.4g
Fibre	1.6g
Sugars	3.1g
Calcium	111mg

Salmon Marinated with Thai Spices

This Scandinavian recipe has been transformed using Thai spices and provides a good source of vitamin D.

INGREDIENTS

Serves 4

tail piece of 1 salmon, about
   675g/1½lb, cleaned and prepared
   (see Cook's Tip)
20ml/4 tsp coarse sea salt
20ml/4 tsp sugar
2.5cm/1in piece fresh root ginger,
   grated
2 lemon grass stalks, coarse outer leaves
   removed, thinly sliced
4 kaffir lime leaves, finely chopped or
   shredded
grated rind of 1 lime
1 fresh red chilli, seeded and
   finely chopped
5ml/1 tsp black peppercorns, coarsely
   crushed
30ml/2 tbsp chopped fresh coriander
coriander and kaffir limes, to garnish

For the coriander and lime dressing
150ml/¼ pint/⅔ cup mayonnaise
juice of ½ lime
10ml/2 tsp chopped fresh coriander

1 Carefully remove all the bones from the salmon (a pair of tweezers is the best tool). Mix together the salt, sugar, ginger, lemon grass, lime leaves, lime rind, chilli, peppercorns and coriander in a bowl.

NUTRITION NOTES

Per portion:

Energy	593kcals/2465kJ
Protein	34.8g
Fat	48.3g
Saturated fat	7.5g
Carbohydrate	5.2g
Fibre	0g
Sugars	5.1g
Calcium	44.8mg

2 Place one quarter of the spice mixture in a shallow dish. Place one fillet, skin down, on top. Spread two-thirds of the remaining mixture over the flesh then place the other fillet on top, flesh down. Sprinkle the rest of the spice mixture over the fish.

COOK'S TIP

Ask your fishmonger to scale the fish, split it lengthways and remove it from the backbone in two matching fillets.

3 Cover the fish with foil, then place a chopping board on top. Add some weights, such as clean cans of fruit. Chill for 2–5 days, turning the fish daily in the spicy brine.

4 Make the dressing by mixing the mayonnaise, lime juice and chopped coriander in a bowl.

5 Scrape the spices off the fish. Slice it as thinly as possible. Serve with the lime dressing, garnished with coriander and wedges of kaffir limes.

MEAT AND POULTRY

Whether it is Irish Stew or Roast Lamb from the Middle East,

lamb is tops when it comes to flavour and texture. One of lamb's

traditional partners is apricots – enjoy the blend of tastes in

Lamb Tagine or Spicy Lamb and Apricots with Pea Rice. Herbs and

spices are wonderful for flavouring chicken dishes such as Chicken

with Lemons and Olives, or Spiced Grilled Poussins – but nothing

could be more aromatic than Chicken with 40 Cloves of Garlic.

Irish Stew

Although you should be trying to cut down on your consumption of red meat, the carrots and onions in this simple and delicious stew provide vital cancer-fighting nutrients. Always try to buy organic meat.

INGREDIENTS

Serves 6
1.2kg/2½lb boneless lamb chops
15ml/1 tbsp vegetable oil
3 large onions, quartered
4 large carrots, thickly sliced
900ml/1½ pints/3¾ cups water
4 large firm potatoes, cut into chunks
1 large thyme sprig
15ml/1 tbsp butter
15ml/1 tbsp chopped fresh parsley
salt and freshly ground black pepper
Savoy cabbage, to serve (optional)

1 Trim any excess fat from the lamb. Heat the oil in a flameproof casserole, add the lamb and brown on both sides. Remove from the pan.

2 Add the onions and carrots to the casserole and cook for 5 minutes. Return the lamb to the pan with the water. Season with salt and pepper. Bring to a boil then reduce the heat, cover and simmer for 1 hour.

3 Add the potatoes to the pan with the thyme, cover again, and simmer for a further hour.

4 Leave the stew to settle for a few minutes. Remove the fat from the liquid with a ladle, then pour off the liquid into a clean saucepan. Bring to a simmer and stir in the butter, then the parsley. Season well and pour back into the casserole. Serve with Savoy cabbage, if liked.

NUTRITION NOTES	
Per portion:	
Energy	968kcals/4095kJ
Protein	93.2g
Fat	49.5g
Saturated fat	20.8g
Carbohydrate	34.1g
Fibre	3.9g
Sugars	7.5g
Calcium	62.5mg

Middle Eastern Roast Lamb and Potatoes

Increase your intake of vitamin E and antioxidants by serving this delicious garlicky lamb with a leafy green vegetable, such as swiss chard or spinach.

INGREDIENTS

Serves 8
2.75kg/6lb leg of lamb
4 garlic cloves, halved
60ml/4 tbsp olive oil
juice of 1 lemon
2–3 saffron strands, soaked in 15ml/
    1 tbsp boiling water
5ml/1 tsp mixed dried herbs
450g/1lb baking potatoes, peeled and
    thickly sliced
2 large onions, thickly sliced
salt and freshly ground black pepper
fresh parsley, to garnish

1 Make eight incisions in the lamb and press in the garlic. Place the lamb in a glass dish. Mix the oil, lemon juice, saffron mixture and herbs. Rub over the lamb, then marinate for 2 hours.

2 Preheat the oven to 180°C/350°F/ Gas 4. Layer the potatoes and onions in a roasting tin. Lift the lamb out of the marinade and place on top of the potatoes and onions, fat side up.

3 Pour any remaining marinade over the lamb and roast for 2 hours, basting occasionally, until the meat is tender. Remove the lamb from the oven, cover loosely with foil and leave to rest in a warm place for about 15 minutes before carving. Serve garnished with fresh parsley.

NUTRITION NOTES	
Per portion:	
Energy	741kcals/3088kJ
Protein	66.7g
Fat	49.2g
Saturated fat	32.8g
Carbohydrate	11.2g
Fibre	1.0g
Sugars	1.4g
Calcium	28.1mg

Lamb Tagine

Combining meat and dried fruit is typical of Middle Eastern cooking. It is also the perfect way to introduce more anti-cancer foods into a meat dish. Dried fruits are full of nutrients, including vitamin C, beta-carotene, potassium and iron.

INGREDIENTS

Serves 4

115g/4oz/½ cup dried apricots
30ml/2 tbsp olive oil
1 large onion, chopped
1kg/2¼lb boneless shoulder of
   lamb, cubed
5ml/1 tsp ground cumin
5ml/1 tsp ground coriander
5ml/1 tsp ground cinnamon
grated rind and juice of ½ orange
5ml/1 tsp saffron strands
15ml/1 tbsp ground almonds
about 300ml/½ pint/1¼ cups lamb or
   chicken stock
5ml/1 tsp sesame seeds
salt and freshly ground black pepper
fresh parsley, to garnish
couscous, to serve

HEALTH BENEFITS

Apricots contain beta-carotene, a powerful antioxidant that is changed to vitamin A in the body. Beta-carotene boosts the immune system and provides oxygen to the cells in the body, helping to fight cancer. Sesame seeds and almonds contain vitamin E, which works in tandem with beta-carotene.

COOK'S TIP

If you do not have time to soak the apricots overnight, use the ready-to-eat variety and add extra stock to replace the soaking liquid.

1 Cut the apricots in half and put in a bowl with 150ml/¼ pint/⅔ cup water. Leave to soak overnight.

2 Preheat the oven to 180°C/350°F/ Gas 4. Heat the olive oil in a flameproof casserole. Add the onion and cook gently for 10 minutes until soft and golden.

3 Stir in the lamb. Add the cumin, coriander and cinnamon, with salt and pepper to taste. Stir to coat the lamb cubes in the spices. Cook, stirring, for 5 minutes.

4 Add the apricots together with their soaking liquid and stir thoroughly. Stir in the orange rind and juice, saffron and ground almonds, then pour over enough stock to just cover the meat.

5 Cover the casserole tightly with a lid and cook in the oven for about 1½ hours until the meat is tender, stirring occasionally. If the tagine appears to be becoming dry, add extra stock during cooking.

6 When the tagine is ready, heat a heavy-based frying pan, add the sesame seeds and dry fry, shaking the pan continuously, until the seeds are golden. Transfer the tagine to a serving dish, sprinkle the sesame seeds over the meat and garnish with fresh parsley. Serve with couscous.

NUTRITION NOTES

Per portion:

Energy	724kcals/3016kJ
Protein	46.8g
Fat	54.1g
Saturated fat	35.7g
Carbohydrate	13.9g
Fibre	2.7g
Sugars	13.5g
Calcium	56.7mg

Spicy Lamb and Apricots with Pea Rice

INGREDIENTS

Serves 4

675g/1½lb leg fillet
15ml/1 tbsp ghee or butter
1 onion, finely chopped
5ml/1 tsp ground coriander
10ml/2 tsp ground cumin
5ml/1 tsp fenugreek
2.5ml/½ tsp turmeric
pinch of cayenne pepper
1 cinnamon stick
120ml/4fl oz/½ cup chicken stock
175g/6oz/¾ cup ready-to-eat apricots
salt and freshly ground black pepper
fresh coriander, to garnish

For the marinade
120ml/4fl oz/½ cup natural yogurt
15ml/1 tbsp sunflower oil
juice of ½ lemon
2.5cm/1in piece root ginger, grated

For the rice
175g/6oz/1 cup chana dhal or yellow
   split peas, soaked for 1–2 hours
225g/8oz/1 cup basmati rice, soaked
15ml/1 tbsp sunflower oil
1 large onion, thinly sliced
1 garlic clove, crushed
10ml/2 tsp finely grated root ginger
5ml/1 tsp turmeric
60ml/4 tbsp natural yogurt
690ml/22fl oz/2¾ cups chicken stock
15ml/1 tbsp chopped fresh coriander
15ml/1 tbsp ghee or butter

1 Cut the meat into bite-size pieces. Mix the marinade ingredients. Add the meat, stir to coat, then cover and leave in a cool place for 2–4 hours.

2 Boil the yellow split peas for 20–30 minutes until tender. Drain well and set aside. Cook the drained rice for 5 minutes. Drain well and set aside.

3 Heat the oil and fry the onion rings for 10–15 minutes until golden. Transfer to a plate. Stir-fry the garlic and ginger for a few seconds, then add the turmeric and yogurt and cook for a few minutes. Add the dhal, coriander and salt, stir well and then remove from the heat and set aside. Preheat the oven to 180°C/350°F/Gas 4.

4 Drain the meat, reserving the marinade. Melt the ghee or butter in a flameproof casserole and fry the onion for 3–4 minutes. Add the spices and fry for 1 minute. Add the meat and fry until browned. Spoon in all the remaining marinade, add the stock and apricots and season well. Bring to the boil, cover and cook in the oven for 45–55 minutes until the meat is tender.

5 Meanwhile, finish cooking the rice. Spoon the dhal mixture into a casserole and stir in the rice. Dot the top with ghee or butter and sprinkle with the onion rings. Cover tightly with a double layer of foil, securing with a lid. Place in the oven about 30 minutes before the lamb is ready. The rice and dhal should be tender, but the grains separate. Serve the rice and spiced lamb garnished with coriander.

— NUTRITION NOTES —	
Per portion:	
Energy	776kcals/3262kJ
Protein	53.3g
Fat	22.6g
Saturated fat	9.9g
Carbohydrate	92.1g
Fibre	5.9g
Sugars	21.8g
Calcium	162.5mg

Chicken with Lemons and Olives

This tangy chicken dish makes a healthy choice, but be sure to buy a free-range or organic chicken that has not been fed with hormones.

INGREDIENTS

Serves 4

2.5ml/½ tsp ground cinnamon
2.5ml/½ tsp ground turmeric
1.5kg/3–3½lb chicken
30ml/2 tbsp olive oil
1 large onion, thinly sliced
5cm/2in piece fresh root ginger, grated
600ml/1 pint/2½ cups chicken stock
2 preserved lemons or limes, or fresh ones, cut into wedges
75g/3oz/¾ cup pitted brown olives
15ml/1 tbsp clear honey
60ml/4 tbsp chopped fresh coriander
salt and freshly ground black pepper
coriander sprigs, to garnish

1 Preheat the oven to 190°C/375°F/ Gas 5. Mix the ground cinnamon and turmeric in a bowl with a little salt and pepper and rub all over the chicken skin to give an even coating.

2 Heat the oil in a large sauté or shallow frying pan and fry the chicken on all sides until it turns golden. Transfer the chicken to an ovenproof dish.

3 Add the sliced onion to the pan and fry for 3 minutes. Stir in the grated ginger and the chicken stock and bring just to the boil. Pour over the chicken, cover with a lid and bake in the oven for 30 minutes.

4 Remove the chicken from the oven, add the lemons or limes and brown olives and drizzle with the honey. Bake, uncovered, for a further 45 minutes until the chicken is tender.

5 Stir in the chopped coriander and season to taste. Garnish with coriander sprigs and serve at once.

NUTRITION NOTES

Per portion:

Energy	375kcals/1580kJ
Protein	57.7g
Fat	14.8g
Saturated fat	4.1g
Carbohydrate	2.8g
Fibre	0.5g
Sugars	2.8g
Calcium	34mg

HEALTH BENEFITS

Olives contain the natural antioxidant vitamin E, which can help fight off the free radicals that damage cells in the body and have the potential to cause cancer.
Vitamin C, found in lemons and limes, has also been found to help combat cancer. Research has also shown that ginger may halt certain cancers.

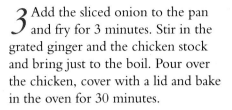

Spiced Grilled Poussins

These tasty poussins are a healthy choice because they contain less fat than red meat.

INGREDIENTS

Serves 4
2 garlic cloves, roughly chopped
5ml/1 tsp ground cumin
5ml/1 tsp ground coriander
pinch of cayenne pepper
1 small onion, chopped
60ml/4 tbsp olive oil
salt
2 poussins
lemon wedges, to garnish

VARIATION

Chicken portions and quail can also be cooked in this way.

---

1 Combine the garlic, cumin, coriander, cayenne pepper, onion, olive oil and salt in a blender or food processor. Process to make a paste that will spread smoothly.

2 Cut the poussins in half lengthways. Place them skin-side up in a shallow dish and spread with the spice paste. Cover and leave to marinate in a cool place for 2 hours.

3 Grill the poussins for about 20 minutes, turning them frequently, until they are cooked and have become crispy on the outside.

4 Serve the poussins immediately, garnished with lemon wedges.

NUTRITION NOTES

Per portion:

Energy	214kcals/891kJ
Protein	19.2g
Fat	15.2g
Saturated fat	2.8g
Carbohydrate	0g
Fibre	0g
Sugars	0g
Calcium	8mg

Chicken with 40 Cloves of Garlic

Garlic is renowned for its healing properties, so this recipe is a "must try" for anyone pursuing an anti-cancer diet.

INGREDIENTS

Serves 6
½ lemon
fresh rosemary sprigs
1.5–1.75kg/3–4½lb chicken
4 or 5 heads of garlic
60ml/4 tbsp olive oil
salt and freshly ground black pepper
steamed broad beans and spring onions,
   to serve

COOK'S TIP

Make sure that each guest receives an equal portion of garlic. They can then mash it into the pan juices for an aromatic sauce.

---

1 Preheat the oven to 190°C/375°F/ Gas 5. Place the lemon half and the rosemary sprigs in the chicken. Separate 3 or 4 of the garlic heads into cloves and remove the papery husks, but do not peel. Slice the top off the other garlic head.

2 Heat the oil in a large flameproof casserole. Add the chicken, turning it in the hot oil to coat the skin completely. Season with salt and pepper and add all the garlic.

3 Cover the casserole with a sheet of foil, then the lid, to seal in the steam and the flavour. Cook for about 1¼ hours until the chicken is cooked.

4 Serve the chicken with the garlic, accompanied by steamed broad beans and spring onions.

NUTRITION NOTES

Per portion:

Energy	316kcals/1326kJ
Protein	40.1g
Fat	15.9g
Saturated fat	3.6g
Carbohydrate	3.4g
Fibre	0.9g
Sugars	0.3g
Calcium	19mg

PASTA, PULSES AND GRAINS

Quick, versatile and easy to cook, pasta is ideal for weekday suppers.

These recipes use a pasta that complements the other ingredients – for

example, Farfalle with Tuna, or spaghetti with Fresh Tomato Sauce.

Pulses and grains are useful store-cupboard ingredients and are the

basis of many nutritious dishes such as dahls and pilaffs. For a

special occasion, try Asian Rice with Fruit and Nuts – a spectacular

and delicious dish from central Asia.

Farfalle with Tuna

Using tuna in this quick and simple dish provides an excellent source of the cancer-fighting nutrients, omega-3 fatty acids and vitamin D.

INGREDIENTS

Serves 6

30ml/2 tbsp olive oil
1 small onion, finely chopped
1 garlic clove, finely chopped
400g/14oz can chopped Italian
   plum tomatoes
45ml/3 tbsp dry white wine
8–10 pitted black olives, cut into rings
10ml/2 tsp chopped fresh oregano or
   5ml/1 tsp dried oregano, plus extra
   fresh oregano to garnish
400g/14oz/3½ cups dried farfalle
175g/6oz can tuna in olive oil
salt and freshly ground black pepper

1 Heat the olive oil in a medium skillet or saucepan, add the onion and garlic and fry gently for about 5 minutes until the onion is soft and lightly coloured.

2 Add the plum tomatoes to the pan and bring to the boil, then add the white wine and simmer for a minute or so. Stir in the olives and oregano, with salt and pepper to taste, then cover and cook for 20–25 minutes, stirring from time to time.

3 Meanwhile, cook the pasta in a large saucepan of salted boiling water according to the instructions on the packet.

4 Drain the canned tuna and flake it with a fork. Add the tuna to the sauce with 60ml/4 tbsp of the water used for cooking the pasta. Taste and adjust the seasoning.

5 Drain the cooked pasta well and tip it into a large, warmed bowl. Pour the tuna sauce over the top and toss to mix. Serve immediately, garnished with sprigs of oregano.

— NUTRITION NOTES —	
Per portion:	
Energy	515kcals/2181kJ
Protein	25.2g
Fat	12.7g
Saturated fat	1.8g
Carbohydrate	78.2g
Fibre	4.2g
Sugars	6.9g
Calcium	54.8mg

Penne with Chicken, Broccoli and Cheese

Broccoli, with its powerful anti-cancer properties, makes a healthy addition to this dish.

INGREDIENTS

Serves 4

115g/4oz/scant 1 cup broccoli florets, divided into tiny sprigs
50g/2oz/¼ cup butter
2 skinless chicken breast fillets, cut into thin strips
2 garlic cloves, crushed
400g/14oz/3½ cups dried penne
120ml/4fl oz/½ cup dry white wine
200ml/7fl oz/scant 1 cup *panna da cucina* or double cream
90g/3½oz/scant 1 cup Gorgonzola cheese, rind removed and diced small
salt and freshly ground black pepper
freshly grated Parmesan cheese, to serve

1 Plunge the broccoli into a saucepan of boiling salted water. Bring back to the boil and boil for 2 minutes, then drain in a colander and refresh under cold running water. Shake well to remove the surplus water and set aside.

2 Melt the butter in a large skillet or saucepan, add the chicken and garlic, with salt and pepper to taste, and stir well. Fry over a medium heat for 3 minutes or until the chicken becomes white. Meanwhile, start cooking the pasta according to the instructions on the packet.

3 Pour the wine and cream over the chicken mixture in the pan, stir to mix, then simmer, stirring occasionally, for about 5 minutes until the sauce has reduced and thickened. Add the broccoli, increase the heat and toss to heat it through and mix it with the chicken. Taste for seasoning.

4 Drain the pasta and tip it into the sauce. Add the Gorgonzola and toss well. Serve with grated Parmesan.

NUTRITION NOTES

Per portion:

Energy	870kcals/3646kJ
Protein	37.7g
Fat	46.1g
Saturated fat	27.4g
Carbohydrate	75.9g
Fibre	3.6g
Sugars	5.1g
Calcium	135.7mg

VARIATION

Use leeks instead of broccoli, which will provide the important nutrient, allium. Fry them with the chicken.

Fresh Tomato Sauce

This famous Neapolitan sauce is full of antioxidants, which can be found in its key ingredients – tomatoes, onions and olive oil. These traditional Mediterranean foods have been shown to lower the incidence of cancer.

INGREDIENTS

Serves 4
675g/1½lb ripe Italian plum tomatoes
60ml/4 tbsp olive oil
1 onion, finely chopped
350g/12oz fresh or dried spaghetti
1 small handful fresh basil leaves
salt and freshly ground black pepper
coarsely shaved Parmesan cheese and
  crusty bread, to serve

1 With a sharp knife, cut a cross in the bottom (flower) end of each tomato. Bring a medium saucepan of water to the boil and remove from the heat. Plunge a few of the tomatoes into the water, leave for 30 seconds, then lift them out with a slotted spoon. Repeat with the remaining tomatoes, then peel off the skin and roughly chop the flesh.

2 Heat the oil in a large saucepan, add the onion and cook over a low heat, stirring frequently, for about 5 minutes until softened and lightly coloured. Add the tomatoes, with salt and pepper to taste, bring to a simmer, then turn the heat down to low and cover. Cook, stirring occasionally, for 30–40 minutes until thick.

3 Meanwhile, cook the pasta according to the instructions on the packet. Shred the basil leaves finely.

4 Remove the sauce from the heat, stir in the basil and taste for seasoning. Drain the pasta, tip it into a warmed bowl, pour the sauce over and toss well. Serve immediately, with shaved Parmesan handed separately.

NUTRITION NOTES

Per portion:

Energy	432kcals/1826kJ
Protein	11.9g
Fat	13.1g
Saturated fat	1.9g
Carbohydrate	71.3g
Fibre	4.4g
Sugars	8.9g
Calcium	37.5mg

VARIATION

Some Neapolitan cooks add a little crushed garlic with the onion and some use chopped fresh oregano or flat leaf parsley with the basil.

Spaghettini with Roasted Garlic

Roasted garlic and olive oil are powerful anti-cancer foods.

INGREDIENTS

Serves 4
1 whole head of garlic
400g/14oz fresh or dried spaghettini
120ml/4fl oz/½ cup extra virgin
  olive oil
salt and freshly ground black pepper
coarsley shaved Parmesan cheese and
  crusty bread, to serve

1 Preheat the oven to 180°C/350°F/ Gas 4. Place the garlic in an oiled baking tin and roast for 30 minutes.

2 Cook the pasta in a saucepan of salted boiling water according to the instructions on the packet.

3 Leave the garlic to cool, then lay it on its side and slice off the top third with a sharp knife.

4 Hold the garlic over a bowl and dig out the flesh from each clove with the point of the knife. When all the flesh has been added to the bowl, pour in the oil and add plenty of black pepper. Mix well.

5 Drain the pasta and return it to the clean pan. Pour in the oil and garlic mixture and toss vigorously over a medium heat until all the strands are thoroughly coated.

6 Serve immediately, with shaved Parmesan handed separately and chunks of bread.

NUTRITION NOTES

Per portion:

Energy	353kcals/1502kJ
Protein	12.9g
Fat	1.8g
Saturated fat	0.2g
Carbohydrate	75.7g
Fibre	3.4g
Sugars	3.5g
Calcium	27mg

VARIATION

For a fiery finish, sprinkle crushed, dried red chillies over the pasta when tossing it with the oil and garlic.

COOK'S TIP

Although you can now buy roasted garlic in supermarkets, it is essential to roast it yourself for this simple recipe, so that it melts into the olive oil and coats the strands of pasta beautifully.

Paglia e Fieno with Radicchio

This light, modern pasta dish is full of wholesome ingredients that will supply the body with valuable nutrients, including antioxidants, phytochemicals, plant protein and fibre.

INGREDIENTS

Serves 4

45ml/3 tbsp pine nuts
350g/12oz dried green and white
   tagliatelle (paglia e fieno)
45ml/3 tbsp extra virgin olive oil
2 pieces drained sun-dried tomatoes in
   olive oil, cut into very thin slivers
30ml/2 tbsp sun-dried tomato paste
40g/1½oz radicchio leaves,
   finely shredded
4–6 spring onions, thinly sliced
   into rings
salt and freshly ground black pepper

1 Put the pine nuts in a non-stick frying pan and toss over a low to medium heat for 1–2 minutes or until they are lightly toasted and golden. Remove and set aside.

2 Cook the pasta according to the packet instructions, keeping the colours separate by using two pans.

— NUTRITION NOTES —	
Per portion:	
Energy	474kcals/1994kJ
Protein	12.6g
Fat	19.6g
Saturated fat	2.1g
Carbohydrate	66g
Fibre	3.1g
Sugars	3.9g
Calcium	35.5mg

3 While the pasta is cooking, heat 15ml/1 tbsp of the oil in a medium-sized skillet or saucepan. Add the sun-dried tomatoes and tomato paste, then stir in about 2 ladlefuls of the water used for cooking the pasta. Simmer until the sauce is slightly reduced, stirring constantly.

4 Mix in the shredded radicchio, taste and season if necessary. Keep on a low heat. Drain the tagliatelle, keeping the colours separate, and return the noodles to the pans in which they were cooked. Add about 15ml/1 tbsp oil to each pan and toss over a medium to high heat until the pasta is glistening with the oil.

5 Arrange a portion of green and white pasta in each of four warmed bowls, then spoon the sun-dried tomato and radicchio mixture in the centre. Sprinkle the spring onions and toasted pine nuts decoratively over the top and serve immediately. Before eating, each diner should toss the sauce ingredients with the pasta so that they mix together.

Tomato and Lentil Dahl with Toasted Almonds

Natural, live yoghurt is not only the perfect accompaniment to this aromatic, antioxidant-rich dish, but is a useful source of healthy bacteria and enzymes.

INGREDIENTS

Serves 4

30ml/2 tbsp vegetable oil
25g/1oz/2 tbsp butter
1 large onion, finely chopped
3 garlic cloves, chopped
1 carrot, diced
10ml/2 tsp cumin seeds
10ml/2 tsp yellow mustard seeds
2.5cm/1in piece fresh root
   ginger, grated
10ml/2 tsp ground turmeric
5ml/1 tsp mild chilli powder
5ml/1 tsp garam masala
225g/8oz/1 cup split red lentils
400ml/14fl oz/1⅔ cups water
400ml/14fl oz/1⅔ cups coconut milk
5 tomatoes, peeled, seeded
   and chopped
juice of 2 limes
60ml/4 tbsp chopped fresh coriander
25g/1oz/¼ cup flaked almonds,
   lightly toasted
salt and freshly ground black pepper

1 Heat the oil and butter in a large heavy-based saucepan, sauté the onion for 5 minutes until softened and lightly coloured, stirring occasionally. Add the garlic, carrot, cumin and mustard seeds and ginger, then cook for 5 minutes, stirring, until the seeds begin to pop and the carrot softens slightly.

2 Stir in the ground turmeric, chilli powder and garam masala, and cook for 1 minute or until the flavours begin to mingle, stirring to prevent the spices burning.

3 Add the lentils, water, coconut milk and tomatoes, then season well. Bring to the boil, then reduce the heat and simmer, covered, for about 45 minutes, stirring occasionally to prevent the lentils sticking.

4 Stir in the lime juice and 45ml/3 tbsp of the fresh coriander, then check the seasoning. Cook for a further 15 minutes until the lentils soften and become tender.

5 Sprinkle with the remaining coriander and the flaked almonds and serve.

— NUTRITION NOTES —	
Per portion:	
Energy	363kcals/1803kJ
Protein	16.1g
Fat	15.6g
Saturated fat	4.7g
Carbohydrate	42.3g
Fibre	4.9g
Sugars	11.4g
Calcium	90mg

Aubergine and Chick-pea Tagine

Ingredients

Serves 4

1 small aubergine, diced
2 courgettes, thickly sliced
60ml/4 tbsp olive oil
1 large onion, sliced
2 garlic cloves, chopped
150g/5oz/2 cups brown cap
  mushrooms, halved
15ml/1 tbsp ground coriander
10ml/2 tsp cumin seeds
15ml/1 tbsp ground cinnamon
10ml/2 tsp ground turmeric
225g/8oz new potatoes, quartered
600ml/1 pint/2½ cups passata
15ml/1 tbsp tomato purée
15ml/1 tbsp chilli sauce
75g/3oz/⅓ cup ready-to-eat
  unsulphured dried apricots
400g/14oz/3 cups canned chick-peas,
  drained and rinsed
salt and freshly ground black pepper
chopped fresh coriander, to garnish
couscous, to serve

1 Sprinkle salt over the aubergine and courgettes and leave for about 30 minutes. Rinse and pat dry with kitchen paper.

2 Heat the grill to high. Arrange the courgettes and aubergine on a baking sheet and toss in 30ml/2 tbsp of the olive oil. Grill for 20 minutes, turning occasionally, until just tender and golden.

3 Meanwhile, heat the remaining oil in a large, heavy-based saucepan and cook the onion and garlic for about 5 minutes until softened, stirring occasionally. Add the mushrooms and sauté for 3 minutes until tender. Add the spices and cook for 1 minute more, stirring, to allow the flavours to mingle.

4 Add the potatoes and cook for 3 minutes, stirring. Pour in the passata, tomato purée and 150ml/¼ pint/⅔ cup water, cover, and cook for 10 minutes or until the sauce begins to thicken.

5 Add the aubergine, courgettes, chilli sauce, apricots and chick-peas. Season, and cook, partially covered, for 10–15 minutes until the potatoes are tender. Add a little extra water if the tagine becomes too dry. Sprinkle with chopped fresh coriander and serve with couscous.

— Nutrition Notes —	
Per portion:	
Energy	338kcals/1425kJ
Protein	12.5g
Fat	14.6g
Saturated fat	1.9g
Carbohydrate	141.7g
Fibre	9.2g
Sugars	16.2g
Calcium	100mg

Bulgur Wheat and Lentil Pilaff

The combination of grains and pulses in this wholesome pilaff make it a good source of plant protein, carbohydrate and fibre – all of which are essential elements in a healthy diet.

INGREDIENTS

Serves 4

115g/4oz/½ cup green lentils
115g/4oz/⅔ cup bulgur wheat
5ml/1 tsp ground coriander
5ml/1 tsp ground cinnamon
15ml/1 tbsp olive oil
225g/8oz rindless streaky bacon
  rashers, chopped
1 red onion, chopped
1 garlic clove, crushed
5ml/1 tsp cumin seeds
30ml/2 tbsp roughly chopped
  fresh parsley
salt and freshly ground black pepper

1 Soak the lentils in cold water for 1 hour and soak the bulgur wheat in boiling water for 15–20 minutes, then drain. Tip the lentils into a pan. Stir in the coriander, cinnamon and 475ml/16fl oz/2 cups water. Bring to the boil, then simmer until the lentils are tender and the liquid has been completely absorbed.

2 Meanwhile, heat the olive oil and fry the bacon until crisp. Remove and drain on kitchen paper. Add the red onion and garlic to the oil remaining in the pan and fry for about 10 minutes until the onion is soft and golden brown. Stir in the cumin seeds and cook for 1 minute more. Return the cooked bacon to the pan.

3 Stir the drained bulgur wheat into the cooked lentils, then add the mixture to the frying pan. Season with salt and pepper and heat through. Stir in the parsley and serve.

COOK'S TIP

Look out for Puy lentils, which have a superior flavour, aroma and texture.

NUTRITION NOTES

Per portion:

Energy	450kcals/1874kJ
Protein	18.2g
Fat	26.0g
Saturated Fat	9.1g
Carbohydrate	37.1g
Fibre	2.8g
Sugars	11.7g
Calcium	41.2mg

Rice and Beans with Avocado Salsa

INGREDIENTS

Serves 4

40g/1½oz/¼ cup dried or 75g/3oz/
  ½ cup canned kidney beans, rinsed
  and drained
4 tomatoes, halved and seeded
2 garlic cloves, chopped
1 onion, sliced
45ml/3 tbsp olive oil
225g/8oz/generous 1 cup long grain
  brown rice, rinsed
600ml/1 pint/2½ cups vegetable stock
2 carrots, diced
75g/3oz/¾ cup green beans
salt and freshly ground black pepper
4 wheat tortillas and soured cream,
  to serve

For the avocado salsa

1 avocado
juice of 1 lime
1 small red onion, diced
1 small red chilli, seeded and chopped
15ml/1 tbsp chopped fresh coriander

1 If using dried kidney beans, soak overnight in cold water. Drain and rinse well. Place in a saucepan with enough water to cover and bring to the boil. Boil rapidly for 10 minutes, then simmer for about 40 minutes until tender. Drain and set aside.

2 Heat the grill. Place the tomatoes, garlic and onion on a baking tray. Toss in 15ml/1 tbsp of the olive oil and grill for 10 minutes or until softened, turning once. Set aside to cool.

3 Heat the remaining oil in a saucepan, add the rice and cook for 2 minutes, stirring, until light golden.

4 Purée the cooled tomatoes and onions in a food processor or blender, then add the mixture to the rice and cook for a further 2 minutes, stirring frequently. Pour in the stock, then cover and cook gently for 20 minutes, stirring occasionally.

5 Reserve 30ml/2 tbsp of the kidney beans for the salsa. Add the rest to the rice mixture with the carrots and green beans and cook for 15 minutes until the vegetables are tender. Season well with salt and pepper. Remove the pan from the heat and leave to stand, covered, for 15 minutes.

6 To make the avocado salsa, cut the avocado in half and remove the stone. Peel and dice the flesh, then toss in the lime juice. Add the onion, chilli, coriander and reserved kidney beans, then season with salt.

7 To serve, spoon the hot rice and beans on to the tortillas. Hand round the salsa and soured cream.

NUTRITION NOTES

Per portion:

Energy	323kcals/1364kJ
Protein	6.8g
Fat	9.7g
Saturated Fat	2.0g
Carbohydrate	55.6g
Fibre	4.7g
Sugars	7.4g
Calcium	46.2mg

HEALTH BENEFITS

Brown rice contains a healthy combination of valuable nutrients, including vitamin E, and helps reduce the risk of bowel cancer.

Asian Rice with Fruit and Nuts

This colourful dish combines rice with nutrient-packed nuts and dried fruits.

INGREDIENTS

Serves 6

75g/3oz/½ cup blanched almonds
60ml/4 tbsp sunflower oil
225g/8oz carrots, cut into julienne strips
2 onions, chopped
115g/4oz/½ cup ready-to-eat unsulphured dried apricots, chopped
50g/2oz/4 tbsp raisins
375g/13oz/scant 2 cups basmati rice, soaked and drained
600ml/1 pint/2½ cups vegetable or chicken stock
150ml/¼ pint/⅔ cup orange juice
grated rind of 1 orange
25g/1oz/⅓ cup pine nuts
salt and freshly ground black pepper
1 red eating apple, cored and chopped

1 Preheat the oven to 160°C/325°F/ Gas 3. Fry the almonds in a shallow pan with a drizzle of the oil for 4–5 minutes until golden in colour.

2 Heat the oil in a heavy ovenproof casserole and fry the carrots and onions over a moderately high heat for 6–8 minutes until both are slightly glazed. Add the apricots, raisins and rice and cook for a few minutes, stirring all the time, until the rice is coated in the oil.

3 Add the stock, orange juice and orange rind, and season well with salt and pepper. Reserve a few almonds and pine nuts to garnish and stir in the remainder. Cover the pan with a double piece of foil and secure with the casserole lid. Cook in the oven for about 30–35 minutes until the rice is tender and all the liquid is absorbed.

4 Remove from the oven and stir in the chopped apple. Spoon on to a warmed serving dish, and then garnish with the reserved almonds and pine nuts. Serve immediately.

NUTRITION NOTES

Per portion:

Energy	689kcals/2870kJ
Protein	13.3g
Fat	26.6g
Saturated fat	2.5g
Carbohydrate	9.9g
Fibre	4.5g
Sugars	22.8g
Calcium	105mg

VARIATION

For a one-dish meal, add about 450g/1lb lamb, cut into cubes. Brown in a little oil and then transfer to a dish and cook the onion and carrots. Return the meat to the casserole with the stock and orange juice.

VEGETABLES AND SALADS

There's nothing quite like health-giving fresh vegetables to enhance dishes. Colour, texture and flavour are the key to these delicious recipes, most of which are suitable for serving on their own as a vegetarian meal, or with meat and fish. For a winter warmer, try Roasted Vegetables with Whole Spice Seeds. And for summer evenings, a colourful Roasted Plum Tomato and Rocket Salad is an ideal accompaniment to barbecued chicken, steak or chops.

Glazed Sweet Potatoes with Ginger and Allspice

These delicious, candied sweet potatoes, with their succulent orange flesh, are full of the vital nutrient, beta-carotene.

INGREDIENTS

Serves 6
900g/2lb sweet potatoes
50g/2oz/¼ cup butter
45ml/3 tbsp oil
2 garlic cloves, crushed
2 pieces of stem ginger, finely chopped
10ml/2 tsp ground allspice
15ml/1 tbsp syrup from ginger jar
10ml/2 tsp chopped fresh thyme, plus a few sprigs to garnish
salt and cayenne pepper

1 Peel the sweet potatoes and cut into 1cm/½in cubes. Melt the butter with the oil in a frying pan. Add the cubes and fry, stirring frequently, for about 10 minutes until just soft.

—— NUTRITION NOTES ——	
Per portion:	
Energy	373kcals/1568kJ
Protein	2.8g
Fat	19.1g
Saturated fat	8.3g
Carbohydrate	50.9g
Fibre	5.4g
Sugars	15.8g
Calcium	56.4mg

2 Stir in the garlic, ginger and allspice. Cook, stirring, for 5 minutes more. Stir in the ginger syrup, salt, a generous pinch of cayenne pepper and the fresh thyme. Stir for 1–2 minutes more, then serve scattered with thyme sprigs.

Roasted Vegetables with Whole Spice Seeds

These crisp, golden vegetables are packed with goodness.

INGREDIENTS

Serves 6
3 parsnips
3 potatoes
3 carrots
3 sweet potatoes
60ml/4 tbsp olive oil
8 shallots, peeled
2 garlic cloves, sliced
10ml/2 tsp white mustard seeds
10ml/2 tsp coriander seeds, lightly crushed
5ml/1 tsp cumin seeds
2 bay leaves
salt and freshly ground black pepper

—— VARIATION ——

Vary the selection of vegetables according to what is available. Try using swede or pumpkin instead of, or as well as, the vegetables suggested.

1 Preheat the oven to 190°C/375°F/ Gas 5. Bring a saucepan of lightly salted water to the boil. Cut the parsnips, potatoes, carrots and sweet potatoes into chunks. Add them to the pan and bring the water back to the boil. Boil for 2 minutes, then drain the vegetables thoroughly.

2 Pour the olive oil into a large, heavy roasting tin and place over a moderate heat. Add the vegetables, shallots and garlic. Fry, tossing the vegetables over the heat until they are pale golden at the edges.

3 Add the mustard seeds, coriander seeds, cumin seeds and bay leaves. Cook for 1 minute, then season with salt and pepper. Transfer the roasting tin to the oven and roast for about 45 minutes, turning occasionally, until the vegetables are crisp and golden and cooked through.

—— NUTRITION NOTES ——	
Per portion:	
Energy	190kcals/793kJ
Protein	2.3g
Fat	11.9g
Saturated fat	1.77g
Carbohydrate	19.6g
Fibre	3.9g
Sugars	6.7g
Calcium	41mg

—— HEALTH BENEFITS ——

Parsnips, carrots and other root vegetables are thought to fight certain cancers.

Spiced Turnips with Spinach and Tomatoes

Sweet baby turnips, tender spinach and ripe tomatoes make a healthful combination in this simple but delicious East Mediterranean vegetable stew. These vegetables are packed with cancer-fighting antioxidants, vitamins and minerals.

INGREDIENTS

Serves 6
450g/1lb plum or other
  well-flavoured tomatoes
60ml/4 tbsp olive oil
2 onions, sliced
450g/1lb baby turnips, topped
  and tailed
5ml/1 tsp paprika
2.5ml/½ tsp sugar
60ml/4 tbsp chopped fresh coriander
450g/1lb fresh young spinach,
  stalks removed
salt and freshly ground black pepper

1 Plunge the tomatoes into a bowl of boiling water for 30 seconds, then refresh in a bowl of cold water. Peel away the tomato skins and chop roughly. Heat the olive oil in a large frying pan or sauté pan and fry the onion slices for about 5 minutes until lightly coloured.

2 Add the baby turnips, tomatoes and paprika to the pan with 60ml/ 4 tbsp water and cook until the tomatoes are pulpy. Cover with a lid and continue cooking until the baby turnips have softened.

3 Stir in the sugar and chopped coriander, then add the spinach, season with a little salt and pepper and cook for a further 2–3 minutes until the spinach has softened and wilted. Serve warm or cold.

NUTRITION NOTES	
Per portion:	
Energy	122kcals/506kJ
Protein	3.5g
Fat	8.4g
Saturated fat	1.2g
Carbohydrate	8.6g
Fibre	4.4g
Sugars	7.9g
Calcium	173.8mg

HEALTH BENEFITS

Turnips are thought to halt the onset of certain cancers. Spinach is an excellent source of cancer-fighting beta-carotene.

Ratatouille

The host of nutritious vegetables used in this traditional Provençal dish make it a delicious and healthful meal in itself, or a valuable addition to any pasta, meat or fish dish.

INGREDIENTS

Serves 6
900g/2lb ripe, well-flavoured tomatoes
120ml/4fl oz/½ cup olive oil
2 onions, thinly sliced
2 red peppers, seeded and cut
　into chunks
1 yellow or orange pepper, seeded and
　cut into chunks
1 large aubergine, cut into chunks
2 courgettes, cut into thick slices
4 garlic cloves, crushed
2 bay leaves
15ml/1 tbsp chopped young thyme
salt and freshly ground black pepper

1 Plunge the tomatoes into boiling water for 30 seconds, then refresh in cold water. Peel away the skins and chop roughly.

2 Heat a little of the oil in a large, heavy-based pan and fry the onions for 5 minutes until soft and golden. Add the peppers and fry for a further 2 minutes. Drain. Add the aubergine and a little more oil and fry gently for 5 minutes. Add the remaining oil and courgettes and fry for 3 minutes. Drain and set aside.

3 Add the garlic and tomatoes to the pan with the bay leaves and thyme and a little salt and pepper. Cook gently until the tomatoes have softened.

NUTRITION NOTES

Per portion:

Energy	191kcals/791kJ
Protein	2.3g
Fat	15.5g
Saturated fat	2.3g
Carbohydrate	11.1g
Fibre	3.1g
Sugars	10.4g
Calcium	26.3mg

COOK'S TIP

There are no specific quantities for the vegetables when making ratatouille so you can, to a large extent, vary the quantities and types of vegetables you choose depending on what you have in the fridge. If the tomatoes are a little tasteless, add 30–45ml/2–3 tbsp tomato purée and a dash of sugar to the mixture along with the tomatoes to add flavour.

4 Return all the vegetables to the pan and cook gently, stirring frequently, for about 15 minutes, until fairly pulpy but retaining a little texture. Season with more salt and pepper to taste.

Spring Vegetable Stir-fry

Fast, fresh and packed with nutrient-rich vegetables, this stir-fry is delicious served with rice or noodles.

INGREDIENTS

Serves 4

15ml/1 tbsp groundnut or vegetable oil
5ml/1 tsp toasted sesame oil
1 garlic clove, chopped
175g/6oz/⅓ cup asparagus tips
2.5cm/1in piece fresh root ginger, finely chopped
225g/8oz/1 cup baby carrots
350g/12oz/3 cups broccoli florets
2 spring onions, cut on the diagonal
175g/6oz/1½ cups spring greens, finely shredded
30ml/2 tbsp light soy sauce
15ml/1 tbsp apple juice
15ml/1 tbsp sesame seeds, toasted

1 Heat a wok or frying pan over a high heat. Add the groundnut or vegetable oil and sesame oil, reduce the heat and sauté the garlic for 2 minutes.

2 Add the asparagus, ginger, carrots and broccoli and stir-fry for 4 minutes. Add the spring onions and spring greens, and stir-fry for a further 2 minutes.

3 Pour over the soy sauce and apple juice and cook for 1–2 minutes until the vegetables are just tender, adding a little water if the stir-fry appears too dry.

4 Sprinkle the sesame seeds on top to serve.

NUTRITION NOTES	
Per portion:	
Energy	109kcals/592kJ
Protein	6.9g
Fat	5.8g
Saturated fat	0.8g
Carbohydrate	7.7g
Fibre	5.9g
Sugars	6.9g
Calcium	174mg

Oriental Green Beans

INGREDIENTS

Serves 4

450g/1lb/3 cups green beans, trimmed
15ml/1 tbsp olive oil
5ml/1 tsp sesame oil
2 garlic cloves, crushed
2.5cm/1in piece fresh root ginger, finely chopped
30ml/2 tbsp dark soy sauce

NUTRITION NOTES	
Per portion:	
Energy	63kcals/259kJ
Protein	2.1g
Fat	4.6g
Saturated fat	0.7g
Carbohydrate	3.6g
Fibre	2.5g
Sugars	2.6g
Calcium	40.7mg

1 Steam the beans for 6 minutes or until just tender.

HEALTH BENEFITS
Green and orange vegetables are an excellent source of beta-carotene, as well as vitamins C and E. When they are lightly cooked with ginger and garlic, they give the immune system a significant boost.

2 Meanwhile, heat the oils in a heavy-based saucepan, and sauté the garlic for about 2 minutes. Add the ginger and soy sauce and cook for a further 2–3 minutes until reduced, then pour over the warm beans.

3 Leave to stand for a few minutes before serving to allow all the flavours to infuse.

Potato Rösti and Tofu with Tomato Sauce

Soya products can play an important role in lowering the risk of cancer. This deliciously flavoursome tofu dish is a natural choice if you want to improve your chances of good health.

INGREDIENTS

Serves 4
425g/15oz/3¾ cups tofu, cut into
   1cm/½in cubes
900g/2lb large potatoes
40g/1½oz/3 tbsp butter, melted
50ml/2fl oz/¼ cup vegetable oil
30ml/2 tbsp sunflower seeds, toasted,
   to serve
salt and freshly ground black pepper

For the marinade
30ml/2 tbsp tamari or dark soy sauce
15ml/1 tbsp clear honey
2 garlic cloves, crushed
4 cm/1½in piece fresh root
   ginger, grated

For the sauce
15ml/1 tbsp olive oil
8 vine-ripened tomatoes, halved,
   seeded and chopped

1 Mix together all the marinade ingredients in a shallow dish and add the tofu. Spoon the marinade over the tofu and leave to marinate in the fridge for at least 1 hour. Turn occasionally to allow the marinade to soak into the tofu.

2 To make the rösti, par-boil the potatoes for 10–15 minutes until almost tender. Leave to cool, then grate coarsely. Season, stir in the melted butter and mix well. Heat half the oil in a large, heavy-based frying pan and divide the potato mixture into four equal portions.

3 Take one quarter of the potato mixture in your hands and form into a rough cake.

4 Place in the pan and flatten the mixture, using your hands or a spatula, to form a round about 1cm/½in thick. Cook for about 6 minutes until golden and crisp underneath. To cook the other side, turn over the rösti by sliding a large plate over the pan and flipping it on to the plate. Gently slide the rösti back into the pan and cook for a further 6 minutes until golden. Cook the remaining rösti in the same way, replenishing the oil when necessary and reserving 30ml/2 tbsp. Keep the rösti warm in a low oven.

5 Heat the remaining oil in the frying pan. Using a slotted spoon, remove the tofu from the marinade and reserve. Fry the tofu for 10 minutes, turning occasionally, until golden and crisp on all sides.

6 To make the sauce, heat the oil in a saucepan, add the reserved marinade and the tomatoes and cook for 2 minutes, stirring. Reduce the heat and simmer, covered, for 10 minutes, stirring occasionally, until the tomatoes break down. Press through a sieve to produce a smooth sauce.

7 To serve, place a rösti on each plate. Arrange the tofu on top. Spoon over the tomato sauce and sprinkle with sunflower seeds.

NUTRITION NOTES

Per portion:

Energy	489kcals/2498kJ
Protein	15.2g
Fat	28.7g
Saturated fat	7.7g
Carbohydrate	44.9g
Fibre	3.8g
Sugars	5.9g
Calcium	567mg

HEALTH BENEFITS

Tofu, or beancurd, is made from processed soya beans and is one of nature's most nutritious foods. There is now evidence to suggest that soya can help to reduce the risk of cancer.

Warm Potato Salad with Herb Dressing

Many herbs are known for their medicinal qualities. The herbs suggested in this delightful salad are commonly used for cleansing and strengthening the body.

INGREDIENTS

Serves 6

1kg/2¼lb waxy or salad potatoes
90ml/6 tbsp extra virgin olive oil
juice of 1 lemon
1 garlic clove, very finely chopped
30ml/2 tbsp chopped fresh herbs, such
  as parsley, basil, thyme or oregano
salt and freshly ground black pepper

1 Cook the potatoes in their skins in boiling salted water.

2 Meanwhile make the dressing. Mix together the olive oil, lemon juice, garlic, herbs and seasoning.

3 Drain the potatoes and leave until cool enough to handle. Peel and cut the potatoes into dice and place in a large bowl.

4 Pour the dressing over the potatoes while they are still warm and mix well. Serve at once, garnished with fresh basil leaves.

NUTRITION NOTES	
Per portion:	
Energy	217kcals/910kJ
Protein	2.9g
Fat	11.5g
Saturated Fat	1.7g
Carbohydrate	26.9g
Fibre	1.9g
Sugars	2.3g
Calcium	20mg

Warm Hazelnut and Pistachio Salad

INGREDIENTS

Serves 4

900g/2lb small new potatoes or
  salad potatoes
30ml/2 tbsp hazelnut or walnut oil
60ml/4 tbsp sunflower oil
juice of 1 lemon
25g/1oz/¼ cup hazelnuts
15 pistachio nuts
salt and freshly ground black pepper
flat leaf parsley sprig, to garnish

NUTRITION NOTES	
Per portion:	
Energy	391kcals/1365kJ
Protein	6.1g
Fat	25.2g
Saturated Fat	2.8g
Carbohydrate	37.2g
Fibre	3.1g
Sugars	33.6g
Calcium	30.7mg

1 Cook the potatoes in their skins in boiling salted water for about 10–15 minutes until tender. Drain well and leave to cool slightly.

2 Meanwhile mix together the hazelnut or walnut oil with the sunflower oil and lemon juice and season well. Pour over the potatoes.

3 Roughly chop the nuts. Sprinkle over the potatoes. Serve garnished with flat leaf parsley.

HEALTH BENEFITS
Nuts and nut oils are a rich source of the valuable antioxidant, vitamin E, which has been associated with lowering the risks of certain types of cancer. Other vital anti-cancer nutrients contained in nuts include vitamin B, calcium and plant protein.

Spinach Salad with Polenta Croûtons

The combination of tender baby spinach leaves, crunchy polenta croûtons and a simple lemon dressing not only makes a delicious tangy salad, but is full of cancer-fighting nutrients.

INGREDIENTS

Serves 4
1 large red onion, cut into wedges
300g/11oz/3 cups ready-made polenta,
    cut into 1cm/½in cubes
olive oil, for brushing
225g/8oz baby spinach leaves
1 avocado, peeled, stoned and sliced
5ml/1 tsp lemon juice

For the dressing
60ml/4 tbsp extra virgin olive oil
juice of ½ lemon
salt and freshly ground black pepper

1 Preheat the oven to 200°C/400°F/ Gas 6. Roast the onion and polenta on lightly oiled baking sheets for about 25 minutes or until the onion is tender and the polenta is golden, turning regularly. Leave to cool slightly.

2 Meanwhile, make the dressing. Combine the olive oil, lemon juice and seasoning in a screw top jar or bowl. Shake or stir to combine.

3 Arrange the spinach leaves in a serving bowl. Toss the avocado slices in the lemon juice to prevent them browning, then add to the spinach with the roasted onions.

4 Pour over the dressing and toss with your hands to combine. Sprinkle over the polenta croûtons just before serving to retain their crunch.

NUTRITION NOTES

Per portion:

Energy	329kcals/1364kJ
Protein	6.1g
Fat	19.7g
Saturated fat	3.2g
Carbohydrate	31.0g
Fibre	3.6g
Sugars	2.5g
Calcium	107.2mg

HEALTH BENEFITS

Corn, from which polenta is made, is thought to help prevent cancer of the colon, breast and prostate. Fresh spinach is a good source of the cancer-fighting nutrient, beta-carotene. Extra virgin olive oil contains the antioxidant vitamin E, while lemon juice contains vitamin C – both of which have been found to help combat cancer.

Roasted Plum Tomato and Rocket Salad

This is a great side salad to accompany grilled chicken or fish and will make an excellent additional source of anti-cancer nutrients in any meal.

INGREDIENTS

Serves 4

225g/8oz/2 cups dried chifferini or
   pipe pasta
450g/1lb ripe baby plum tomatoes,
   halved lengthways
75ml/5 tbsp extra virgin olive oil
2 garlic cloves, cut into thin slivers
30ml/2 tbsp balsamic vinegar
2 pieces sun-dried tomato in olive oil,
   drained and chopped
large pinch of sugar, to taste
1 handful rocket, about 65g/2½oz
salt and freshly ground black pepper

1 Preheat the oven to 190°C/375°F/ Gas 5. Meanwhile, cook the pasta in salted boiling water according to the instructions on the packet.

2 Arrange the halved tomatoes cut side up in a roasting tin, drizzle 30ml/2 tbsp of the oil over them and sprinkle with the slivers of garlic and salt and pepper to taste. Roast in the oven for 20 minutes, turning once.

3 Put the remaining oil in a large bowl with the vinegar, sun-dried tomatoes, sugar and a little salt and pepper to taste. Stir well to mix. Drain the pasta, add it to the bowl of dressing and toss to mix. Add the roasted tomatoes and mix gently.

4 Before serving, add the rocket, toss lightly and taste for seasoning. Serve at room temperature or, alternatively, chilled.

HEALTH BENEFITS

Tomatoes contain the bioflavonoid, lycopene, which is believed to prevent some forms of cancer by reducing the harmful effects of free radicals.

NUTRITION NOTES

Per portion:

Energy	352kcals/1480kJ
Protein	8.2g
Fat	16.6g
Saturated fat	2.4g
Carbohydrate	45.4g
Fibre	3.1g
Sugars	5.5g
Calcium	54.8mg

VARIATION

• If you are in a hurry and don't have time to roast the tomatoes, you can leave out the roasting step and make the salad with halved raw tomatoes instead.
• If you like, add 150g/5oz/1¼ cups mozzarella cheese, drained and diced, with the rocket in Step 4.

Watercress, Pear, Walnut and Roquefort Salad

Combining fresh, raw fruit and salad leaves with walnuts creates a delicious cleansing salad that is rich in antioxidants and enzymes that boost the immune system.

INGREDIENTS

Serves 6
75g/3oz/½ cup shelled walnuts, halved
2 red Williams pears
15ml/1 tbsp lemon juice
150g/5oz/1 large bunch watercress,
    tough stalks removed
200g/7oz/2 scant cups Roquefort, cut
    into chunks

For the dressing
45ml/3 tbsp extra virgin olive oil
30ml/2 tbsp lemon juice
2.5ml/½ tsp clear honey
5ml/1 tsp Dijon mustard
salt and freshly ground black pepper

1 Toast the walnuts in a dry frying pan for 2 minutes until golden, tossing frequently to prevent them from burning.

2 Meanwhile, make the dressing. Combine the olive oil, lemon juice, honey, mustard and seasoning in a screw-top jar or bowl. Shake or mix to combine thoroughly.

3 Halve the pears, remove the cores, then cut into slices. Toss the pear slices in the lemon juice to prevent them browning, then combine with the watercress, walnuts and Roquefort in a bowl.

4 Pour the dressing over the salad, toss well and serve immediately.

NUTRITION NOTES	
Per portion:	
Energy	287kcals/1189kJ
Protein	9.3g
Fat	38.0g
Saturated Fat	8.5g
Carbohydrate	5.9g
Fibre	1.9g
Sugars	5.8g
Calcium	237mg

Panzanella

This classic Tuscan salad brings together nutrient-packed raw vegetables with open-textured Italian bread.

INGREDIENTS

Serves 6
275g/10oz/10 slices day-old Italian-
    style bread, thickly sliced
1 medium cucumber, peeled and cut
    into chunks
5 tomatoes, seeded and diced
1 large red onion, chopped
225g/8oz/1⅓ cups good quality olives
20 basil leaves, torn

For the dressing
60ml/4 tbsp extra virgin olive oil
15ml/1 tbsp red or white wine vinegar
salt and freshly ground black pepper

1 Soak the bread in water for about 2 minutes, then remove and squeeze gently, first with your hands and then in a tea towel to remove any excess water. Store in the fridge for 1 hour.

2 Meanwhile, make the dressing. Place the oil, vinegar and seasoning in a screw-top jar or bowl. Shake or mix to combine.

3 Mix together the cucumber, tomatoes, onion and olives in a large serving bowl. Break the bread into chunks and add to the bowl with the torn basil leaves. Pour the dressing over the salad, and toss lightly to combine. Serve immediately.

NUTRITION NOTES	
Per portion:	
Energy	219kcals/918kJ
Protein	4.9g
Fat	11.4g
Saturated Fat	1.6g
Carbohydrate	25.9g
Fibre	2.2g
Sugars	3.8g
Calcium	75.8mg

DESSERTS, BREADS AND BAKES

This section includes some ideas for delicious fruity desserts. Date, Fig and Orange Pudding is the ideal winter pudding, while in summer you can enjoy a simple Mango and Orange Sorbet, or impress your dinner guests with an Exotic Fruit Salad with Passion Fruit Dressing. Here too, are some wholesome and tasty breads, and two teatime treats – Date and Walnut Brownies and a wonderful Ginger Cake.

Date, Fig and Orange Pudding

Fresh orange juice and rind gives this light and tangy steamed pudding a nutritious citrus kick.

INGREDIENTS

Serves 6

juice and grated rind of 2 oranges
115g/4oz/⅔ cup stoned, ready-to-eat
    dried dates, chopped
115g/4oz/⅔ cup ready-to-eat dried
    figs, chopped
175g/6oz/¾ cup unsalted butter, plus
    extra for greasing
175g/6oz/¾ cup soft light brown sugar
3 eggs
75g/3oz/⅔ cup self-raising
    wholemeal flour
115g/4oz/1 cup unbleached
    self-raising flour
30ml/2 tbsp golden syrup
strips of orange rind for decoration

1 Put the orange juice and rind into a saucepan. Add the dates and figs. Cook, covered, over a gentle heat for 8–10 minutes, until soft. Leave to cool, then purée in a blender until smooth.

2 Cream the butter and sugar until pale and fluffy, then beat in the fig purée. Beat in the eggs, then fold in the flours and mix until combined.

3 Grease a 900ml/1½ pint/3¾ cup pudding basin, and pour in the golden syrup. Tilt the bowl to cover the inside with a layer of syrup, or use a spatula.

4 Spoon the pudding mixture into the basin. Cover with greaseproof paper, with a pleat down the centre, and then with pleated foil, and tie down tightly with string.

5 Place the bowl in a large saucepan, and pour in enough water to come halfway up the sides of the bowl. Cover with a tight-fitting lid and steam for 2 hours. Check the water occasionally and top up, if necessary. Turn out and decorate with the strips of orange rind.

HEALTH BENEFITS

Dried fruit is packed with concentrated nutrients, including iron, potassium, calcium, phosphorus, beta-carotene, some B vitamins and vitamin C.

NUTRITION NOTES

Per portion:

Energy	581kcals/2439kJ
Protein	8.7g
Fat	28.0g
Saturated fat	16.9g
Carbohydrate	80.1g
Fibre	3.9g
Sugars	58.1g
Calcium	168mg

Summer Pudding

This classic pudding is made with red summer berry fruits, which are rich in antioxidants, carotenes and vitamins C and E.

INGREDIENTS

Serves 4

8 × 1cm/½in-thick slices of day-old white bread, crusts removed
800g/1¾lb/6–7 cups mixed berry fruit, such as blackberries, raspberries, blackcurrants, redcurrants and blueberries
50g/2oz/¼ cup golden caster sugar
lightly whipped double cream or crème fraîche, to serve

1 Trim a slice of bread to fit in the base of a 1.2 litre/2 pint/5 cup pudding basin, then trim another 5–6 slices and carefully line the sides of the basin.

2 Place all the fruit in a saucepan with the sugar. Cook gently for 4–5 minutes until the juices begin to run – it will not be necessary to add any water. Allow the mixture to cool, then spoon the berries and enough of their juices to moisten the bread into the pudding basin. Save any leftover juice to serve with the pudding.

3 Fold over the excess bread, then cover the fruit with the remaining bread slices, trimming them to fit. Place a small plate or saucer directly on top of the pudding, fitting it inside the basin. Weight it down with a 900g/2lb weight if you have one, or use a couple of full cans as weights.

4 Leave the pudding in the fridge for at least 8 hours or overnight. To serve, run a knife between the pudding and the basin and turn it out on to a plate. Spoon any reserved juices over the top and serve with whipped cream or crème fraîche.

HEALTH BENEFITS

Berries and currants are rich in antioxidant nutrients that can inhibit the growth of cancer cells and protect against cell damage by carcinogens.

NUTRITION NOTES

Per portion:

Energy	266kcals/1125kJ
Protein	7.4g
Fat	1.5g
Saturated fat	0.25g
Carbohydrate	59.3g
Fibre	3.2g
Sugars	26.9g
Calcium	110mg

Mango and Orange Sorbet

This gloriously vibrant sorbet not only makes a refreshing end to a meal, but will give you an extra boost of vital nutrients.

INGREDIENTS

Serves 4
115g/4oz/generous ½ cup golden
   unrefined caster sugar
300ml/½ pint/1¼ cups water
2 large mangoes, peeled, stoned
   and diced
juice of 1 orange
1 free-range egg white (optional)
thinly pared strips of fresh unwaxed
   orange rind, to decorate

1 Place the sugar and water in a saucepan and gently heat until all the sugar is dissolved. Bring to the boil, then reduce the heat and simmer for about 5 minutes. Leave to cool.

2 Put the mango flesh, orange juice and sugar syrup in a food processor and blend until smooth.

3 Pour the mixture into a shallow freezer-proof container and freeze for 2 hours until semi-frozen. Whisk the egg white, if using, until it forms stiff peaks, then stir it into the mixture. Whisk well to remove any ice crystals and return to the freezer until solid.

4 Transfer the sorbet to the fridge 10 minutes before serving to soften. Serve, decorated with orange rind.

HEALTH BENEFITS

Mangoes and oranges aid the digestion, boost the immune system and are said to cleanse the blood.

NUTRITION NOTES

Per portion:

Energy	148kcals/632kJ
Protein	0.8g
Fat	0.1g
Saturated fat	0g
Carbohydrate	39.1g
Fibre	1.7g
Sugars	38.9g
Calcium	25.3mg

Rhubarb and Ginger Yogurt Ice

This low-fat alternative to ice cream is based on creamy fromage frais and live yogurt, which provide healthy bacteria and enzymes.

INGREDIENTS

Serves 6
200g/7oz/scant 1 cup fromage frais
300g/11oz/scant 1½ cups set natural
   live yogurt
375g/13oz/3 cups rhubarb, trimmed
   and chopped
45ml/3 tbsp stem ginger syrup
30ml/2 tbsp clear honey
3 pieces stem ginger, finely chopped

1 Whisk together the fromage frais and yogurt, then pour into a shallow freezer-proof container and freeze for 1 hour.

2 Put the rhubarb, stem ginger syrup and honey in a saucepan and cook over a low heat for 15 minutes, or until the rhubarb is soft. Leave to cool, then purée in a blender or food processor.

3 Fold the rhubarb and stem ginger into the semi-frozen yogurt mixture and beat well. Return to the freezer and freeze for a further 2 hours.

4 Beat again, then freeze until solid. Transfer to the fridge to soften 15 minutes before serving.

HEALTH BENEFITS

Yogurt contains bacteria that is thought to help prevent cancer of the colon.

NUTRITION NOTES

Per portion:

Energy	107kcals/451kJ
Protein	5.4g
Fat	2.8g
Saturated fat	1.7g
Carbohydrate	15.8g
Fibre	0.9g
Sugars	15.8g
Calcium	184mg

Melon Trio with Ginger Biscuits

Fresh melon and ginger are both powerful anti-cancer foods, brimming with goodness, which makes this eye-catching dessert a refreshing and healthy choice.

INGREDIENTS

Serves 4
¼ watermelon
½ honeydew melon
½ Charentais melon
60ml/4 tbsp stem ginger syrup

For the biscuits
25g/1oz/2 tbsp unsalted butter
25g/1oz/2 tbsp caster sugar
5ml/1 tsp clear honey
25g/1oz/¼ cup plain flour
25g/1oz/¼ cup mixed glacé fruit, finely chopped
1 piece of stem ginger in syrup, drained and finely chopped
30ml/2 tbsp flaked almonds

1 Remove the seeds from the melons, cut them into wedges, then slice off the rind. Cut all the flesh into chunks and mix in a bowl. Stir in the ginger syrup, cover and chill until ready to serve.

2 Meanwhile, make the biscuits. Preheat the oven to 180°C/350°F/ Gas 4. Melt the butter, sugar and honey in a saucepan. Remove from the heat and stir in the remaining ingredients.

3 Line a baking sheet with non-stick baking paper. Space four spoonfuls of the mixture on the paper at regular intervals, leaving plenty of room for spreading. Flatten the mixture slightly into rounds and bake for 15 minutes or until the tops are golden.

4 Let the biscuits cool on the baking sheet for 1 minute, then lift each one in turn, using a fish slice, and drape over a rolling pin to cool and harden. Repeat with the remaining ginger mixture to make eight biscuits in all.

5 Serve the melon chunks with some of the syrup and the ginger biscuits.

NUTRITION NOTES

Per portion:

Energy	219kcals/919kJ
Protein	2.6g
Fat	9.5g
Saturated fat	3.7g
Carbohydrate	32.5g
Fibre	1.3g
Sugars	27.5g
Calcium	45mg

COOK'S TIP

For an even prettier effect, scoop the melon flesh into balls with the large end of a melon baller.

Exotic Fruit Salad with Passion Fruit Dressing

Made of exotic fruits that are particularly rich in beta-carotene, this tangy fruit salad makes an excellent antioxidant dessert.

INGREDIENTS

Serves 6
1 mango
1 papaya
2 kiwi fruit
coconut or vanilla ice cream, to serve

For the dressing
3 passion fruit
thinly pared rind and juice of 1 lime
5ml/1 tsp hazelnut or walnut oil
15ml/1 tbsp clear honey

1 Peel the mango, cut it into three slices around the stone, then cut the flesh into chunks and place in a large bowl. Peel the papaya and cut it in half. Scoop out the seeds, then chop the flesh and add to the bowl.

2 Cut both ends off each kiwi fruit, then stand them on a board. Using a small, sharp knife, cut off the skin from top to bottom. Cut each kiwi fruit in half lengthways, then cut into thick slices and add to the bowl.

3 To make the dressing, cut each passion fruit in half and scoop out the seeds into a sieve set over a small bowl. Press the seeds well with the back of a spoon to extract all their juices. Lightly whisk the lime juice, hazelnut or walnut oil and honey into the passion fruit juice, then pour the dressing over the fruit and mix gently.

4 Cover, then transfer to the fridge to chill for 1 hour. Serve with scoops of coconut or vanilla ice cream.

COOK'S TIP

A clear, golden honey scented with orange blossom or acacia blossom would be perfect for the dressing.

HEALTH BENEFITS

Mango, papaya and kiwi fruit contain the anti-cancer nutrient, beta-carotene.

NUTRITION NOTES

Per portion:

Energy	46.8kcals/198kJ
Protein	0.7g
Fat	1.0g
Saturated fat	0g
Carbohydrate	9.3g
Fibre	1.6g
Sugars	9.2g
Calcium	13mg

Spicy Millet Bread

Enjoy all the nutrients of millet in this delicious spicy bread. Eat it warm, straight from the oven, with a thick winter soup.

INGREDIENTS

Makes 1 loaf
90g/3½oz/½ cup millet
550g/1lb 6oz/5½ cups strong plain
  flour
10ml/2 tsp salt
5ml/1 tsp sugar
5ml/1 tsp dried chilli flakes (optional)
10g/¼oz sachet easy-blend dried yeast
350ml/12fl oz/1½ cups warm water
25g/1oz/2 tbsp butter
1 onion, roughly chopped
15ml/1 tbsp cumin seeds
5ml/1 tsp ground turmeric

1 Bring 200ml/7fl oz/scant 1 cup water to the boil, add the millet, cover and simmer gently for 20 minutes until the grains are soft and the water is absorbed. Remove from the heat and leave to cool until just warm.

2 Mix together the flour, salt, sugar, chilli flakes, if using, and yeast in a large bowl. Stir in the cooked millet, then add the warm water and mix to form a soft dough.

3 Turn out on to a floured work surface and knead for 10 minutes until smooth and elastic.

4 Place in an oiled bowl and cover with oiled clear film or a dish towel. Leave to rise in a warm place for 1 hour until doubled in size.

5 Melt the butter in a heavy-based frying pan and fry the onion for 10 minutes until softened, stirring occasionally. Add the cumin and turmeric, and fry for 5–8 minutes longer, stirring constantly, until the cumin seeds begin to pop. Set aside.

6 Knock back the dough by pressing down with your knuckles to deflate the dough, then shape it into a round. Spoon the onion mixture into the middle of the dough, bringing the sides over the filling to make a parcel. Seal the parcel well.

7 Place the loaf on an oiled baking sheet, seam-side down, cover with oiled cling film and leave in a warm place for 45 minutes until doubled in bulk. Meanwhile, preheat the oven to 220°C/425°F/Gas 7.

8 Bake the bread for 30 minutes until golden. Check the bread is fully cooked by tapping on its underside – it should sound hollow. Leave to cool on a wire rack.

HEALTH BENEFITS

Millet is often associated with bird food. However, it is a versatile grain and, if eaten on a regular basis as part of a varied diet, can help lower the risk of certain cancers.

NUTRITION NOTES

Per loaf:

Energy	2400kcals/10156kJ
Protein	57.8g
Fat	29.3g
Saturated fat	14.8g
Carbohydrate	499.9g
Fibre	17.9g
Sugars	11.9g
Calcium	825mg

COOK'S TIP

To test if a dough has risen, make a small indentation in the top with your index finger. If the indentation does not spring back entirely, rising is complete; if it springs back at once, the dough is not ready.

Sweet Potato Bread with Cinnamon and Walnuts

This is a wonderful brunch dish, packed with cancer-fighting beta-carotene and antioxidants.

INGREDIENTS

Makes a 900g/2lb loaf
1 sweet potato
5ml/1 tsp ground cinnamon
450g/1lb/4 cups strong white flour
5ml/1 tsp easy-blend dried yeast
50g/2oz/⅓ cup walnut pieces
300ml/½ pint/1¼ cups warmed milk
salt and freshly ground black pepper

COOK'S TIP

For an extra-crispy loaf, after the bread is cooked, remove from the tin and return the bread to the oven for 5 minutes, placing it upside down on the oven rack.

1 Boil the whole potato in its skin for 45 minutes or until tender.

2 Meanwhile, sift the cinnamon and flour together into a large bowl. Stir in the yeast, and season.

3 Drain the potato and cool in cold water, then peel off the skin. Mash the potato with a fork and mix into the dry ingredients with the nuts.

4 Make a well in the centre and pour in the milk. Bring the mixture together with a round-bladed knife.

5 Turn out the dough on to a floured surface. Knead for 5 minutes. Return the dough to a bowl and cover with a damp cloth. Leave to rise for about 1 hour or until doubled in size.

6 Turn the dough out and knock back to remove any air bubbles. Knead again for a few minutes. If the dough feels sticky add a little more flour to the mixture. Shape into a ball and place the bread in an oiled and base-lined 900g/2lb loaf tin. Cover with a damp cloth and leave to rise in a warm place for about 1 hour or until doubled in size.

7 Preheat the oven to 200°C/400°F/ Gas 6. Bake the bread on the middle shelf of the oven for 25 minutes. Turn out the bread and tap the base; if it sounds hollow the bread is cooked. Cool on a wire rack.

NUTRITION NOTES

Per loaf:

Energy	2147kcals/9087kJ
Protein	61.3g
Fat	45.3g
Saturated fat	6.8g
Carbohydrate	398.3g
Fibre	18.3g
Sugars	31.6g
Calcium	1073mg

Wholemeal Sunflower Bread

Sunflower seeds provide an extra helping of nutrients in this delightfully nutty wholemeal loaf. It is delicious served with a chunk of cheese and a rich tomato chutney.

INGREDIENTS

Serves 6

450g/1lb/4 cups strong
    wholemeal flour
2.5ml/½ tsp easy-blend dried yeast
2.5ml/½ tsp salt
50g/2oz/½ cup sunflower seeds, plus
    extra for sprinkling
300ml/½ pint/1¼ cups warm water

1 Mix together the flour, yeast, salt and sunflower seeds in a large bowl. Make a well in the centre and gradually stir in the warm water. Mix vigorously with a wooden spoon to form a soft, sticky dough.

2 Cover with a damp dish towel and leave to rise in a warm place for 45–50 minutes until doubled in size.

NUTRITION NOTES

Per portion:

Energy	272kcals/1189kJ
Protein	11.1g
Fat	5.6g
Saturated fat	0.6g
Carbohydrate	49.4g
Fibre	7.3g
Sugars	1.7g
Calcium	37.6mg

3 Preheat the oven to 200°C/400°F/ Gas 6. Turn the dough out on to a floured work surface and knead for 10 minutes – the dough will still be quite sticky to touch.

--- HEALTH BENEFITS ---

Sunflower seeds are extremely high in the cancer-fighting antioxidant, vitamin E.

4 Form the dough into a rectangle and place in a 450g/1lb greased and lightly floured loaf tin. Sprinkle the top with sunflower seeds. Cover with a damp cloth and leave to rise again for a further 15 minutes.

5 Bake for 40–45 minutes until golden – the loaf should sound hollow when tapped underneath. Leave to cool on a wire rack.

Banana and Pecan Bread

This extra-moist teabread can make a healthy treat. Bananas are full of nutrients, and pecans nuts are a great anti-cancer food.

INGREDIENTS

Makes a 900g/2lb loaf
115g/4oz/½ cup butter, softened
175g/6oz/⅔ cup light muscovado sugar
2 large eggs, beaten
3 ripe bananas
75g/3oz/¾ cup pecan nuts, coarsely chopped
225g/8oz/2 cups self-raising flour
2.5ml/½ tsp ground mixed spice

COOK'S TIP

If the mixture shows signs of curdling when you add the eggs, stir in a little of the flour to stabilize it.

1 Preheat the oven to 180°C/350°F/ Gas 4. Generously grease a 900g/ 2lb loaf tin and line it with non-stick baking paper. Cream the butter and muscovado sugar in a large mixing bowl until the mixture is light and fluffy. Gradually add the eggs, beating after each addition, until well combined.

2 Peel and then mash the bananas with a fork. Add them to the creamed mixture with the chopped pecan nuts. Beat until well combined.

3 Sift the flour and mixed spice together and fold into the banana mixture. Spoon into the tin, level the surface and bake for 1–1¼ hours or until a skewer inserted into the middle of the loaf comes out clean. Cool for 10 minutes in the tin, then invert the tin on a wire rack. Lift off the tin, peel off the lining paper and leave to cool completely.

NUTRITION NOTES

Per loaf:

Energy	3220kcals/13520kJ
Protein	45.8g
Fat	163.3g
Saturated fat	71.6g
Carbohydrate	419.7g
Fibre	13.3g
Sugars	245.3g
Calcium	952mg

Date and Walnut Brownies

These rich, sticky brownies are great for afternoon tea. They are packed with nutrients, including vitamin C, antioxidants, soluble fibre and potassium.

INGREDIENTS

Makes 12
350g/12oz plain chocolate, broken into squares
225g/8oz/1 cup butter, diced
3 large eggs
115g/4oz/generous ½ cup caster sugar
5ml/1 tsp pure vanilla essence
75g/3oz/⅔ cup plain flour, sifted
225g/8oz/1½ cups fresh dates, peeled, stoned and chopped
200g/7oz/1¾ cups walnut pieces
icing sugar, for dusting

1 Preheat the oven to 190°C/375°F/ Gas 5. Generously grease a shallow 30 × 20cm/12 × 8in baking tin and line with non-stick baking paper.

2 Put the chocolate and butter in a large, heatproof bowl. Place the bowl over a pan of hot water and leave to melt. Stir until smooth, then lift the bowl out and cool slightly.

3 Beat the eggs, sugar and vanilla in a separate bowl. Then beat into the chocolate mixture, and fold in the flour, dates and nuts. Pour into the tin.

4 Bake for 30–40 minutes until firm. Cool in the tin. Turn out, remove the paper and dust with icing sugar.

NUTRITION NOTES

Per portion:

Energy	505kcals/2106kJ
Protein	6.7g
Fat	36.7g
Saturated fat	10.6g
Carbohydrate	39.7g
Fibre	1.7g
Sugars	34.5g
Calcium	50.8mg

Ginger Cake

Three forms of cancer-fighting ginger make this the ultimate cake for all lovers of the spice.

INGREDIENTS

Makes 12 squares

225g/8oz/2 cups self-raising flour
15ml/1 tbsp ground ginger
5ml/1 tsp ground cinnamon
2.5ml/½ tsp bicarbonate of soda
115g/4oz/½ cup butter
115g/4oz/½ cup soft light brown sugar
2 eggs
25ml/1½ tbsp golden syrup
25ml/1½ tbsp milk

For the topping

6 pieces stem ginger, plus 20ml/4 tsp
  syrup, from the jar
115g/4oz/1 cup icing sugar
lemon juice

1 Preheat the oven to 160°C/325°F/ Gas 3. Grease a shallow 18cm/7in square cake tin and line with non-stick baking paper.

2 Sift the flour, ginger, cinnamon and bicarbonate of soda into a bowl. Rub in the butter, then stir in the sugar. Make a well in the centre.

3 In a bowl, whisk together the eggs, syrup and milk. Pour into the dry ingredients and beat until smooth and glossy.

4 Spoon into the prepared tin and bake for 45–50 minutes until well risen and firm to the touch. Leave in the tin for 30 minutes, then remove to a wire rack to cool completely.

5 For the topping, cut each piece of stem ginger into quarters and arrange the pieces on top of the cake.

6 Sift the icing sugar into a bowl and stir in the ginger syrup and enough lemon juice to make a smooth icing. Put into a greaseproof paper icing bag and drizzle over the top of the cake. Leave to set, then cut into squares.

--- NUTRITION NOTES ---

Per portion:

Energy	189kcals/936kJ
Protein	3.0g
Fat	9.2g
Saturated fat	5.6g
Carbohydrate	34.5g
Fibre	0.5g
Sugars	20.5g
Calcium	79.9mg

--- COOK'S TIP ---

This cake benefits from being kept in an airtight tin for a day before eating.

Information File

CONTACTS FOR PERSONAL SUPPORT

Bacup
3 Bath Place
Rivington Street
London EC2A 3JR
Tel: 0171 613 2121

British Association for Counselling
1 Regent Place
Rugby
Warwickshire CV21 2PJ
Tel: 01788 550899

British Cancer Help Centre
Grove House
Cornwallis Grove
Clifton
Bristol BS8 4PG
Tel: 0117 980 9505

Gerson Therapy Information
(The Debra Shepherd Trust)
Chapel Farm
West Humble
Dorking
Surrey RH5 6AY
Tel: 01306 882865

Institute for Optimum Nutrition
Blades Court
Deodar Road
London SW15 2NU
Tel: 0181 877 9993

Council for Complementary and Alternative Medicine
Suite 1
19a Cavendish Square
London W1M 9AD
Tel: 0171 409 1440

Sivananda Yoga Vedanta Centre
51 Felsham Road
London SW15 1AZ
Tel: 0181 780 0160

The Soil Association
86 Colston Street
Bristol BS1 5BB
Tel: 01179 290661

Organic Gardening
Ryton-on-Dunsmore
Coventry CV8 3LG
Tel: 01203 303517

Cancer Society of New Zealand
PO Box 1724
Auckland
New Zealand
Tel: (09) 524 2628

Canadian Cancer Society
10 Alcorn Avenue
Toronto
Ontario M4V 3B1
Tel: (01) 416 961 7223

Australian Cancer Society
PO Box 4708
Sydney 2001
Tel: (61) 2267 1944

ORGANIC FOODS AND REMEDIES

Cantassium Direct
225 Putney Bridge Road
London SW15
Tel: 0181 874 1130

Organics Direct
Ledbury
Herefordshire
Tel: 0171 729 2828

Neal's Yard Remedies and East West Herbs
Neal's Yard
London WC2H 9DP
Tel: 0171 379 7662

JOURNALS

Positive Health
521 Queen Square
Bristol, BS1 4LJ
Tel: 0117 983 8851

Caduceus (Healing into Wholeness)
38 Russell Terrace
Leamington Spa
Warwickshire CV31 1HE
Tel: 01926 451897

Journal of Alternative and Complementary Medicine
Green Library
9 Rickett Street
London SW6 1RU
Tel: 0171 385 4566

BOOKS

Bishop, Beata, *A Time to Heal* (Hodder & Stoughton, 1985; reprinted by Penguin Arcana Range, 1996)

Brown, S. and Fletcher, D., *Vital Touch – Japanese Do-In Exercises* (The Community Health Foundation, 1991)

Chamberlain, Jonathan, *Fighting Cancer – A Survival Guide (An A–Z of Cancer Treatment Options)* (Headline, 1997)

Erasmus, U., *Fats that Heal, Fats that Kill* (Alive Books, Burnaby, BC, Canada, 1993)

Faulkner, Dr Hugh, *Against All Odds* (The Community Health Foundation, 1992)

Gerson, M., *A Cancer Therapy – Results of 50 Cases* (Totality Books, Del Mar, CA, USA, 1977)

Goodman, Sandra, *Nutrition and Cancer* (Green Library Publications, 1998)

Holford, Patrick, *The Optimum Nutrition Bible* (Piatkus, 1998)

Holford, Patrick, *100% Health* (Piatkus, 1998)

Lichfield, Clive, *The Organic Directory 1999–2000* (Green Earth Books, 1998)

Passwater, Richard A., *The Antioxidants* (Keats Publishing Inc, Connecticut, 1997)

Simonton, O. Carl, S. Matthews-Simonton, S. and Creighton, J. L., *Getting Well Again* (Bantam Books, 1986)

Walker, N.W., *Fresh Vegetable and Fruit Juices* (Norwalk Press, 1978)

Wigmore, Ann, *The Sprouting Book* (Avery Publishing Group Inc, 1986)

Wigmore, Ann, *The Wheatgrass Book* (Avery Publishing Group Inc, 1985)

Index

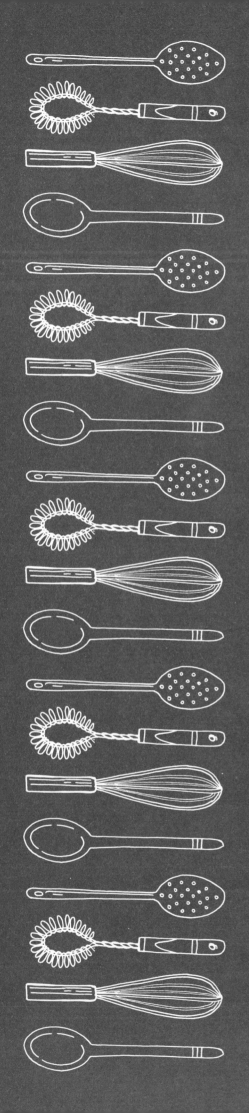